Organizational
Team
Building

WINTHROP MANAGEMENT SERIES

William H. Brickner, *Series Editor*

BRICKNER AND COPE

The Planning Process

CAMPBELL

Understanding Information Systems: Foundations for Control

ENDS AND PAGE

Organizational Team Building

ROCKEY

Communicating in Organizations

SANFORD AND ADELMAN

Management Decisions: A Behavioral Approach

SCHAEFER

The Motivation Process

Organizational
Team
Building

Earl J. Ends
Curtis W. Page

Winthrop Publishers, Inc.
Cambridge, Massachusetts

Library of Congress Cataloging in Publication Data

Ends, Earl J
   Organizational team building.

   (Winthrop management series)
   Includes bibliographies.
   1. Management. 2. Work groups. 3. Organiza-
tion. I. Page, Curtis W., joint author. II. Title.
HD38.E465   658.4   77-4694
ISBN 0-87626-627-8

Cover illustration by Ruth Williams.

Photographs by David T. Farrell.

© 1977 by Winthrop Publishers, Inc.
  17 Dunster Street, Cambridge, Massachusetts 02138

10 9 8 7 6 5 4 3 2 1

contents

two

three

four

five

editor's preface

Energy crisis! Political crisis! Personal crisis! Economic crisis! . . . . I believe they all have a common element: *mismanagement*. It may be mismanagement of resources, mismanagement of everyday activities, mismanagement of organizations large and small, or mismanagement of societies in general; however, it is becoming increasingly clear that many people do not manage well.

If we define management as planning and using resources such as time, money, energy, etc. to attain stated objectives (goals), then the ability to manage well can have a significant impact on almost every life experience. We conceived the Winthrop Management Series with the idea that the basic skills and principles necessary for successful managing are not complicated; almost anyone can learn them. With a basic understanding of these skills and principles, people can become more effective managers at all levels: in large organizations, in small groups, or in their personal lives.

WHO NEEDS 'EM? (MORE BOOKS ON MANAGEMENT, THAT IS)

We have directed the books in this series primarily toward those people who would like to do a better job of managing, yet who have neither the time nor the inclination to enroll in a full program of management courses at the university

ix

level. The authors have written the books to be used individually, or as a set, in industrial training programs, community colleges, university extension classes, or as focused
readings in undergraduate or graduate management courses.
In addition, the authors hope that the books will provide
useful self-study material for those people who learn on their
own by reading daily.

Organizations in all areas of society are growing larger
and more complex. As a result, individuals with a wide
variety of backgrounds and vocations are recognizing the
need to learn the principles of good management. Hopefully
they can benefit from the Winthrop Management Series. Experienced professional managers also may see these volumes
as an aid in successfully carrying out one of the most important managerial duties, that of helping subordinates to manage
their jobs more effectively.

WHAT THIS SERIES IS ABOUT

The books in the series are concerned with those skills which
experienced managers find most critical for developing a
successful managerial career. The results of a nationwide
questionnaire to 266 top and middle managers in business,
government, and nonprofit organizations are shown in the
following table. The managers ranked these skills and per-

Skills		*Personal Attributes*	
Leadership and Motivation	18.7%*	Ability to Work with Others	22.5%*
Information Systems	11.6%	Drive, Energy	21.7%
Communication	11.2%	Adaptability to Change	11.9%
Understanding Human Behavior	10.8%	Intellectual Capacity	11.9%
Finance	10.4%	Ability to Communicate	10.4%
Awareness of Environment	7.1%	Integrity	8.4%
Planning	6.4%		

*Shows relative weight assigned from 100% total.

sonal attributes as most important for long-term managerial success in the future.[1] Accordingly, the authors have examined many of these skills and attributes in these six series volumes:

1. *The Planning Process* by Brickner and Cope.
2. *Understanding Information Systems: Foundations for Control* by Campbell.
3. *Organizational Team Building* by Ends and Page.
4. *Communicating in Organizations* by Rockey.
5. *Management Decisions: A Behavioral Approach* by Sanford and Adelman.
6. *The Motivation Process* by Schaefer.

Communication, decision making, and the ability to motivate oneself and others are process skills important to all managers. The books on planning, organization building, and control through information systems include the most important functions that managers perform. Although the six books do not discuss all of the many topics involved in management, we feel that they cover the most important ones.

MAJOR SERIES THEMES

One of the main themes of the Winthrop Management Series is the concept of *systems* or *processes*. Management is not a series of unrelated activities. Like the universe, management is an interlocking rational system governed by "laws." The fact that many of these laws are "undiscovered" should not detract from the principle that management is an ongoing process. This process involves inputs of resources and infor-

[1] Brickner, W.H. *The Managers of Today Look at Those of Tomorrow*. Presented at the National Meeting of the Academy of Management, Seattle, Wash., August, 1974.

mation, the shape and form of which are changed, resulting in some outcome. Information about the outcome (feedback) is then compared with the desired outcome (objective). If the comparison is unsatisfactory, the inputs or the processor are changed. The following diagram illustrates this concept:

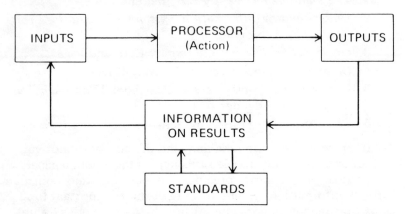

Each of the topics covered in this series is actually a smaller system, or process, that is a part of the overall system of management.

Another key concept in organizing the material for these books is *Pareto's Law*. This "law" states that a relatively small percentage of the inputs creates a large percentage of the outcomes. (For example, 20 percent of a firm's customers may be responsible for 80 percent of its sales volume.) With regard to the series, each author has organized each book around a few specific ideas which he or she believes to be the major keys for successfully mastering each basic process discussed.

The application of principles and theories to real-world situations is an extremely difficult problem for many people. To help bridge the gap between theory and practice, each volume contains a *Panel Discussion* of several successful management practitioners. They are individuals with varied backgrounds who in their careers have successfully used whatever management process they were talking about. The panelists addressed themselves to the problems and opportunities which could result from applying the theories discussed by the author in the preceding chapter of the book. The resulting dialogues are rich in insights and guides that can aid both novice and experienced managers.

ACKNOWLEDGMENTS

Many people have been involved in the creation of the Winthrop Management Series. However, one person above all made it possible. My personal gratitude goes to Michael Meehan, our editor at Winthrop Publishers, Inc. Mike provided early encouragement when the series was but a faint idea. Subsequently as this idea became more tangible, he was willing to "put his money where his mouth is" and support the publishing of the six volumes.

The help which these books will provide to managers is the result of the unstinting efforts of a creative team of authors and panelists, each of whom contributed to the series the knowledge of a lifetime of managerial experience. They all took time out from very busy professional lives to share this knowledge with others. My thanks to each of them.

William H. Brickner
Series Editor
Los Altos, California

authors' preface

This book is intended to be a primer on the skill of organizational team building. Based upon our experience with many hundreds of managers enrolled in Pepperdine University's School of Business and Management MBA programs, and our experience as consultants to a broad variety of clients in the business community, we have been convinced for some time that team building is one of the most important, most neglected, and least understood parts of a manager's job. The most common reason for neglecting team building appears to be the assumption that it is a talent you are born with or without—if you don't have it, you somehow must learn to manage without it. But an overwhelming amount of data proves beyond any doubt that the assumption is false. Team building is a skill, not an innate talent. This is a crucial distinction because skills are learned. As a consequence, we have approached team building as a learnable skill.

Like most highly valued skills, team building is a complex skill comprising many simple component skills. We have attempted to unravel the complex skill of team building and identify its components. But skills are learned by doing, not by reading about them, so we have attempted to describe just what it is that you must do to acquire team-building skills.

We recognize that skills are learned by people who want to learn them; the learner must provide the initiative. Therefore we have tried to point out the limitless opportunities available to learn team-building skills, provided that you take the initiative to do so.

To the extent that we have succeeded in doing what we set out to do, the text will have a distinctly "do-it-yourself" flavor. We sincerely hope you will make the most of it.

If we have succeeded in making the process of organizational team building understandable, we owe a debt of gratitude to hundreds of students and client managers. Over the years they have forced us to abandon much of the academic and scientific jargon of psychology and organizational behavior and explain what we were talking about in basic English. We hope that in our attempt to communicate simply and clearly, our efforts will not be misread as oversimplification. This is, after all, intended to be a primer. The true graduate course must be taken in the real world of business, not in the classroom.

We also wish to express our appreciation to members of our discussion panel: Shirley Chilton, Walter Kruel, Robert Covington, and David Farrell. We believe the insights they provided from the perspective of top management have added immeasurably to the "real-world" orientation of the text. We regret that page limitations did not permit inclusion of the entire panel discussion. However, we hope the portions presented here will give you a fair idea of how key executives view the importance of team building.

Earl J. Ends
Curtis W. Page

Organizational
Team
Building

one

The Nature of Organizations

OBJECTIVES

After reading Chapter One you should be able to:

1. Describe the dual nature of business organizations.
2. Discuss the purpose, structure, and processes of the formal organization.
3. Describe the purpose, structure, and processes of the informal organization.
4. Identify the manager's role in the organization.

INTRODUCTION

A manager is a person who fulfills a very special role in an organization. To provide an understanding of the managerial role, in this chapter we will discuss two major topics. First we will briefly examine the dual nature of a business organization; then we will discuss the four basic functions of management.

THE DUAL NATURE OF AN ORGANIZATION

In its simplest form, a business organization consists of a group of people who are organized to work together in order to provide some service and/or product for sale at a price that yields an acceptable return for the effort, investment, and risk incurred. This definition contains the three basic characteristics of any organization: a purpose, a structure, and a process. However, because organizations are made up of people, and people are social animals by nature, virtually all organizations are really two organizations in one: a formal organization and an informal organization. This dual nature requires that, if we are to understand what an organization is all about and what a manager's job really is, then we must consider a minimum of two purposes, two structures, and two processes. We can think of the formal organization as the official one—the one described by organization charts, job descriptions, administrative policy and procedure manuals, and work procedures. These describe how the whole organization is intended to operate in order to achieve its purpose. We can think of the informal organization as the social system which inevitably emerges whenever people spend much time together. This organization is not described in any company manual, indeed it is often not evident to the casual observer, yet it is a very real fact of life that every manager must cope with, for if the purpose, structure, and processes of the informal organization are significantly out of tune with those of the formal organization, the enterprise is in serious trouble. Let us examine these concepts in greater detail.

THE FORMAL ORGANIZATION

The Purpose of the Formal Organization

While exceptions can always be found, the primary reason a business exists at all is to provide income for its owners and employees. A business organization can be regarded as a useful mechanism for combining the effort, knowledge, skill, and capital of a group of people to produce some service or product which is sold, thereby generating income for all members of the group.

Development of the Formal Organization Structure

If a manager were to depend completely on the kind of organization that spontaneously emerges when people are thrown together, the odds are that the organization would not survive very long or get very much accomplished. To deal with this problem, virtually any group established for some specific purpose, such as manufacturing and selling widgets or putting on the Fourth of July picnic, finds it necessary to develop a *formal organization*. This simply means that duties have been assigned to the various people involved and that relationships among them have been specified: who are "Chiefs"; who are "Indians"; who collects the money; who signs the checks; who sweeps the floor. By adding up all the duties and responsibilities assigned to each person in the group, one winds up with a role definition, or job description, for each member of the group. Thus a formal organization is a scheme for assigning roles as well as duties. It should be apparent that with different roles go different amounts of status, even though some duties may be shared. For example, a gas station mechanic has more status than the pump jockey, even though both pump gas during rush periods. The station manager, in turn, has higher status than the mechanic because the definition of the manager's role includes the right to hire and fire mechanics. The full definition of any role includes a statement of its relation to any other role in an organization.

The manager's higher status does not solely derive from the greater authority the manager has, but also from the much greater responsibility. The manager is responsible for a number of decisions that influence the viability of the enterprise. He or she may decide whether to extend credit to certain customers, what merchandise to stock, how much part-time help is needed, and many other things. The mechanic, on the other hand, has responsibilities as well. The mechanic must decide which jobs to take, what parts to order, and when the work can be completed, as well as providing estimates of how much it will cost, and so forth. The pump jockey probably makes no decisions that affect the business; however, the way that person does the job may have a considerable effect on the business because if employees are courteous, friendly, and cheerful, then customers are more likely to return than if they are not. Similarly, the mechanic must turn out competent work to keep customers satisfied. And the manager must supervise employees to make sure that they live up to the organization's expectations and those of the customers. In turn, the employees also expect certain things from the manager. They expect to be paid on time, they expect to be treated fairly, and so on. Gradually these expectations become part of the role definition of the person from whom such behavior is expected.

Most organizations sooner or later find it necessary to develop rules that are designed to keep people operating within their assigned roles and to maintain the formal relations between roles. For example, one rule might be that no one but the manager can extend credit to a customer, another that no one but the mechanic can accept a repair job or promise when it will be done. Other rules might be that the manager will have paychecks available for pickup at 10 A.M. every Thursday, or that the pump jockey will assist the mechanic when asked to do so. Some of the rules cover the formal reward and punishment system of the organization. For example, anyone caught stealing from the company is automatically fired; employees are entitled to buy their tires at a 20 percent discount; after a full year on the job, employees are entitled to one week vacation with pay.

In summary, the structure of the formal organization can be defined in terms of the various job roles it sponsors, the relations among those roles, and the rules that are designed to keep people operating within those formal roles. Formal roles, relations, and rules are all designed to ensure that the needs of the formal organization are met by specifying what part each member is supposed to play in achieving the purpose of the group and what rewards and punishments adhere to conforming with the rules or breaking them. Though not as common as it used to be, one rule designed to maintain the formal structure is that one cannot talk to a higher-level manager about a problem or complaint unless first having discussed it with one's immediate supervisor and gotten that person's express permission to carry the matter further up the management hierarchy.

Development of the Formal Organizational Process

Closely related to the development of the formal structure is the development of the formal process. In fact, structure and process are highly interdependent. While the structure tells who the players are, how much authority and responsibility they have, and what they are each supposed to do, process deals with how all of these activities fit together. The activities of all the various members in the fulfillment of their roles must somehow be coordinated so that related activities occur in the right sequence. The activities must also be integrated to make sure that all bases are covered and no resources are wasted. Coordination occurs between a manufacturing manager and a sales manager when the sales manager checks with the manufacturing manager before promising a customer a delivery date on a big order. Failure to do so may result in an angry customer and loss of business, as well as in hostility between the two managers. The importance of integration is most easily understood from an example of the lack of it. Suppose your class had decided to put on a dance for the freshman class. Arrangements were made for advertising and for renting and decorating the hall, tickets were sold, money collected. When the big night arrived, it was suddenly discovered that no one was specifically assigned the responsibility for hiring the band: That is lack of integration. Or just as bad from a financial point of view, suppose two committee members each took it upon themselves to hire a band of their choice. The dance might be a huge success from a fun point of view, but it might also be a financial disaster. That, too, illustrates lack of integration of the activities of the organization.

As organizations grow most find it useful to record the critical internal and external processes of the organization in the form of written procedures and/or flow diagrams. These devices record, for example, how an order for a product taken by a sales representative eventually results in receipt of a check from the customer for goods received. In small organizations, the formal process may entail only a few distinct steps, perhaps only ten or twelve. In a large organization hundreds of steps involving many people and many departments may be involved. Figure 1-1 is an example of a flow

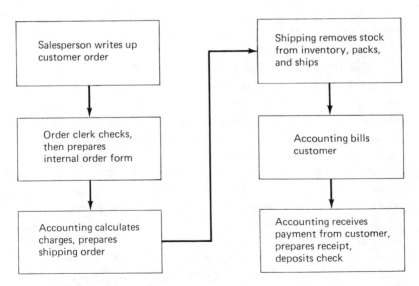

Figure 1-1. Simplified Example of a Flow Design for Processing an Order

diagram. Table 1-1 outlines an example of a written procedure. Both are ways of designating (if the organization has
been in existence for some time) the processes that an
organization uses to manufacture a product, to do its cost
accounting, to figure its payroll, and to perform all the other
processes necessary to carry on business. Whether recorded
or not, all organizations have some formal processes which
ensure that the work moves smoothly from department to
department and from person to person through the organization. Ideally all these processes should fit together like a giant
jigsaw puzzle with all the pieces in place. They are the glue
that ties all the people together and enables them to collec-
tively achieve the goals or purposes of the organization.

THE INFORMAL ORGANIZATION

The Purpose of the Informal Organization

The purpose of the informal, or social, organization is
simply to satisfy the personal needs of individual members of
the organization. It evolves so spontaneously and so naturally
that most people are not even aware that they are developing
a social organization. The development of the informal system begins with individuals, who may be strangers, all trying
to satisfy their individual needs. Some will make out very
well because they possess better interpersonal and group
skills than do others. As a consequence, the informal organization does not have a single purpose, but rather a collection of individual purposes, some of which are achieved and
many of which are not. The more skillful may achieve their
purposes at the expense of the less skillful, leading to frustration and the development of hostilities. Or, in the pursuit of
need satisfaction, people may form subgroups to increase

Table 1-1. Simplified Example of a Written Procedure
for Processing an Order

---

1. Salesperson writes up customer order and turns in customer order to Sales Department order clerk.
2. Order clerk checks stock number, quantity, price, weight, destination, shipping instructions.
3. Order clerk prepares internal order form and sends to Accounting Department.
4. Accounting Department, on receipt of order, checks customer credit, calculates discount if applicable, calculates shipping costs, prepares shipping order, and sends order to Shipping Department.
5. Shipping Department withdraws material from inventory, corrects inventory records, prepares for shipping per instructions, notifies carrier to pick up shipment, gets receipt from carrier, returns receipt and copy of shipping order to Accounting Department.
6. Accounting Department bills customer, enters amount due in Accounts Receivable, receives check from customer (or sends second request), credits customer Accounts Receivable, deposits check.

---

their power to satisfy their personal needs. This too can result in conflict among subgroups. Meanwhile, the purpose of the formal organization may be completely forgotten by many of its members. The organization may become a very unpleasant place to work. On the other hand, with effective managerial leadership these same forces can be channelled to ensure a more equitable distribution of personal need satisfaction. When this happens, both individuals and the organization benefit.

Development of the Informal Organization Structure

Whenever a number of people find themselves in frequent contact for extended periods of time—for any purpose—some sort of social organization begins to develop. This simply means that the persons involved begin to establish patterns of behavior toward each other that are associated with living and working together. For example, in a typical college class, by the middle of the semester a social organization has clearly begun to emerge. Likes and dislikes have developed. Friendships and conflicts have been initiated. Behavioral norms defining acceptable and unacceptable behavior in the class have evolved. Subgroups may have formed. Individual roles such as the class "brain," the class "clown," or the discussion "leader" may have emerged. Group expectations are formed about each person's performance, behavior, attitudes, and feelings with respect to the group's purpose and with respect to other group members. The course of development of the social organization will have a considerable effect on how well the formal purpose of the organization is served. For example, if several small but hostile subgroups develop within a class, so much class time may be wasted by subtle game playing, one-upsmanship, and the like, that very little actual learning takes place. The subgroups in conflict have placed their own personal needs for status above the needs of the organization, the class as a whole in this case, and have seriously jeopardized the chances of fulfilling its purpose. As a consequence, everyone loses.

The effective teacher recognizes that he or she can exert considerable influence on the emerging social organization in the classroom; indeed, often the teacher must do so to prevent disastrous outcomes. Such problems are not confined to the classroom. Similar conflict occurs in all organizations simply because people are people. The social system of an organization is an ever-present fact of life that the manager must recognize and cope with. Fortunately, as we shall see in subsequent chapters, the effective, skillful manager can and must exert considerable influence on the course of evolution of the social system in the organization. This is true whether one is managing only five people or five thousand.

When people accept a job in a business organization, they bring with them their own personal sets of needs. No two individuals have exactly the same set, yet each individual will attempt to satisfy as many personal needs as possible on the job. In fact, unless at least some of an employee's personal needs are met, that person usually exerts very little effort to satisfy the needs of the organization that provides his or her livelihood. The human needs that are of primary importance in business can be divided into three broad categories: economic, psychological, and social. In this section we will consider only the social needs because they seem to exert the greatest influence on the informal organization.

One major social need is *the need for attention and approval*. We want others to notice us and approve of what we are doing. We want to feel that others consider us worthy of their attention. We want them to recognize us as unique human beings who are capable of making a worthwhile contribution to the organization. As Eric Berne says in his book on transactional analysis (a form of psychotherapy), everyone needs stroking to keep from shriveling up and dying inside. *Positive stroking* is the transactional analysis term for a compliment, for a thank you, for an approving smile, or for some other form of favorable recognition or consideration. Some people have much greater needs of this kind than do others. But everybody needs some attention and approval, and few receive as much as they would like.

Another significant social need is *the need to belong and conform*. In essence, this is the need to fit in with and be liked by others. Any effort a manager puts into helping employees pull together rather than apart is well spent. One of the many important payoffs in team building derives from the fact that a strong team helps individual members satisfy this basic need. To be a good team member, one must conform to the rules of the team. This is a very powerful need in most people because if one does not belong, one has little opportunity to satisfy one's need for attention and approval.

A third important social need is *the need to participate and contribute*. We all have the need to be involved in something we feel is worthwhile. The feeling of involvement arises not only from wanting to participate and contribute, but also from the sense that others welcome your participation and contribution to the group effort. Thus all three social needs are interdependent. *Unless you belong you don't have a chance to participate and contribute. If you don't partici- pate and contribute, you not only do not belong, but you also gain no opportunity to satisfy your need for attention and approval.* Interestingly enough, effective team building helps all team members meet these three basic social needs.

Many studies of businesses have shown that employees will find a way of satisfying their social needs no matter how hard management tries to thwart them. Most of the frustra- tion of these needs by management is based more on ignor- ance of their importance than on deliberate attempts to block their satisfaction. Nevertheless, if a manager does not make sure that at least some of these social needs can be sat- isfied in a way that supports the goals of the organization, they are likely to be satisfied in ways that will reduce the productivity and profitability of the organization. But more about that later.

In summary, the structure of the informal organization is defined by the roles which the group allows individual mem- bers to assume. It is based on personal influence among mem- bers of the group; the pecking order that is established; who likes whom, who dislikes whom; religious, political, and ethnic prejudices, and a lot of other things. As these social roles in the group become more firmly established, the in- formal organization develops its own system of rewards and punishments. And it may have a greater influence on em- ployees' behavior than does the formal organization.

Development of the Informal Organization Process

As suggested earlier, the informal or social processes al- ways develop when a group of people are in frequent contact.

They result simply because people will see to it that at least some of their personal needs are met whenever the opportunity arises. Since the average person spends about one-third of his or her waking hours on the job, it seems only reasonable that people take advantage of that time to satisfy some of their personal needs. As discussed earlier, *the emergence of the informal structure of the organization is one result of the pursuit of personal need satisfaction.* Just as the informal structure may interfere with the intended workings of the formal structure, the informal processes may interfere with the smooth workings of the formal processes of the organization.

The informal processes can occur at three levels: the interpersonal level, the group level, and the intergroup level.

THE INTERPERSONAL LEVEL

The *interpersonal level* of processes is illustrated in the following example involving an executive secretary. While part of her formal job is to screen callers and subordinates who want appointments to see the boss, effective salespeople and subordinates alike have learned that the executive secretary is a *very important person.* Not only does she control access to the executive, but she can often influence the boss's response to the person who does get an appointment. Those who treat the executive secretary like an unimportant clerk may find they will have a long wait for an appointment. Or subordinates may find that the boss has a negative attitude toward them when they are admitted. The executive secretary can subtly influence the boss's behavior even by such casual remarks as, "Mr. Smith from accounting has been after me all week to see you. He has some scheme for running your department better. Do you *really* want to see him, or shall I tell him you're too busy? Your schedule is loaded with really important things that only you can handle, you know." Whatever his scheme, the odds are that it will never fly, even if he does eventually get to see the boss. Mr. Smith made the mistake of alienating the executive secretary, treating her as though she were a mere typist. Mr. Smith failed to recognize her high status in the informal organization. As a result the legitimate formal process assigned to the executive secretary, that of screening and making appointments, has been distorted and used by her to satisfy her personal needs.

On the other hand, suppose sales representative Don Jones wants to try to sell the company some new equipment. Having dealt with many executive secretaries in his successful career, he knows how they expect to be treated. He first establishes a friendly relationship, by sincere use of complimentary conversation, for example, recognizing her tasteful grooming, the importance of her job, or whatever seems appropriate. Her social status duly recognized, some of her personal needs are met. Therefore when Jones asks for the appointment, the odds are that he gets one (even if it means cancelling out Mr. Smith from the Accounting Department).

The nature of the interpersonal relationship between two people can greatly influence how much useful work gets done. It also determines whether either will receive any personal need satisfaction from the relationship. For example, suppose two people working at an electronic assembly bench intensely dislike each other. Suzy Smith's job is to rivet several small transformers and relays to the chassis. She then passes the chassis to Sally Grimes, who makes the wiring connections and solders them, then passes them back to Suzy, who rivets on several more parts. Then Suzy passes them to a third person for the next operation. Because Suzy and Sally don't like each other, they both try hard to make each other look bad and thereby make themselves look good. The hostility started when Suzy first came to work and heard Sally comment to another employee that, "They always put the dumb ones on riveting." Unsure of herself anyway because she was new on the job, that remark was a blow to Suzy's ego. To make matters worse, Sally was very fast and kept prodding Suzy for holding up her work and being a slow-poke. Normally, Sally's soldering job took the same amount of time as Suzy's two fastening operations on the chassis, but as Suzy's resentment continued to get stronger, she began looking for ways to get even. She discovered that if she "accidently" bent, kinked, or unravelled the stranded lead wires in a certain way, it took Sally much longer to do the soldering because she had to take time to straighten, unkink, or retwist the wires first. This slowed down production by 10 percent. Suzy added fuel to the fire by making several snide remarks to Sally. Not to be outdone, Sally soon discovered that if she bent and soldered the wires in a certain way, it took Suzy much longer to perform her second riveting operation. Suzy had to bend them out of the way to keep them from being damaged by the riveting operation. This slowed production down another 10 percent.

The literature is full of examples like those above. Nearly anyone who has worked in an organization—whether a business, a governmental agency, or even a volunteer organization—has witnessed or been party to such informal processes. The variety is endless. However, it should not be assumed that informal processes are always negative in effect. As we shall see later, the manager can greatly influence the direction the informal processes take.

THE GROUP LEVEL

The *group level* informal process is usually referred to as *group dynamics*. As is the case with interpersonal dynamics, they can work for or against the organization. In other words, groups can pull together, or they can pull apart. If they pull together, they can either pull for or against the organization as a whole. One example of a group pulling apart was a small cost-accounting department in a large mining company located in the Canadian wilderness. The group was made up mostly of young people only one or two years out of college, and one senior "oldtimer". For over a year, the group never met any of its deadlines without massive and continual use of overtime. Overtime was required two or three nights a week, all day Saturday, and often on Sunday. The quality of the work was poor and work often had to be redone. The senior employee, Hans, spent most of his time locating and correcting errors others had made. He believed and frequently stated that they were all incompetent. The younger employees hated the older man because he made them feel inferior by continually pointing out their errors. Besides their hatred of Hans, they agreed only on the futility of their work, that the company was a terrible place to work, and that all management was incompetent. They were constantly complaining and bickering among themselves and always tried to blame someone else for errors discovered. None of them felt any obligation to improve the quality of their work. Even though the entire town contained only 7,000 people, the employees never got together socially. Their supervisor, the department manager, spent most of his time in the office putting together reports for upper management. Other than when signing overtime authorizations, he rarely saw them or spoke to them.

Fortunately the same group can be used to illustrate pulling together for the organization. This came about because an MBA student needed a behavioral term project. With the manager's permission, the student (also an accountant) decided to apply team-building techniques to cope with the problem. After one meeting during which he listened to employees ventilate their complaints for three hours, he proposed that as a group task they perform a management system analysis of the cost-accounting department operation. This involved preparing flow diagrams of all internal processes within the department, tracing all inputs to their original sources, and tracing all outputs to their ultimate users. By eliminating reports that no longer were used by anybody, the employees were able to eliminate overtime entirely within two weeks. In addition, they found that they had enough spare time to expand the cost-accounting function into new areas. Group morale and cohesiveness grew steadily. By the end of the second month, with the help of Hans, whom they now respected, they uncovered a situation that had allowed a contractor to overcharge the company $10,000 per month for over eighteen months. Needless to say, management corrected the situation immediately and rewarded the cost accountants, and the MBA student was promoted to Department Manager by the end of the year.

The most common examples of groups pulling together against the purpose of the organization are from factories and construction projects. The group agree among themselves to restrict the amount of work they will do and woe betide the group member who violates the rule. The usual purpose is to force management to provide overtime in order to meet schedules. Sometimes, however, employee unity merely reflects workers' hostility toward management or their fear of working themselves out of a job.

THE INTERGROUP LEVEL

The *intergroup level* of informal process can be illustrated by the conflict between the Research and Development En-

gineering Department (R&D) and the Production Engineering
Department (PE) in a medium-size manufacturing plant.
R&D had the responsibility for developing new products and
designing items to meet customer requirements. After the
design was completed and several samples built and tested,
the design drawings were turned over to PE. PE was supposed
to make production drawings of every part for use by the
various machine operators, and to specify how the parts
would be assembled and tested. Where possible, they were
also to be on the lookout for ways to save money in the
manufacturing process by proposing minor design changes
that did not affect performance of the item. Whenever the
PE engineers found a way of simplifying the design or reducing its manufacturing cost, they initiated an Engineering
Change Notice (ECN), which went first to the PE Department Manager for approval, then to the R&D Department for
an engineering analysis of the proposed change to make sure
it did not affect the performance and quality of the product.
The formal intergroup procedure required that R&D prepare
a formal report on the effect of the change on the product
and a recommendation for acceptance or rejection of the
change. These were then submitted to the Director of Engineering for final authorization if the change was accepted.
If the change was rejected, the manager of the PE Department, if he felt strongly about it, could appeal to the Director of Engineering. Then a joint meeting would be called and
a decision thrashed out. While few rejections were appealed,
the process of generating ECN's cost about $1,000 each, on
the average, for all the engineering and drafting time involved.
The R&D manager and the PE manager were constantly at
each others' throats and wasted most of the Engineering
Director's staff meeting time hurling accusations of incompe-
tence at one another. The conflict between the two managers
had been going on for over five years. Engineers in the two
groups feuded as much as their managers—and with the tacit
approval of their bosses. R&D engineers felt that they were

the elite group who kept the company in business by inventing and developing new products. They referred to the PE engineers as "correspondence school engineers" and "glorified draftsmen". The PE engineers bitterly resented the high status, high pay scale, and special privileges of the R&D engineers. They referred to the R&D engineers as "incompetent, overpaid prima donnas" and devoted a considerable amount of their time and ingenuity trying to find fault with R&D designs. This effort resulted in a constant flood of proposed ECNs. An analysis of the proposed ECNs revealed that over 90 percent were without any merit at all. Through intervention with organization development methods (see Chapter Five) the conflict between the departments and the managers was finally resolved. As one result, the flood of ECNs without merit—that is, those motivated simply by an attempt to make R&D look bad—slowed to a trickle. The savings effected the first year the organizational development program was in effect was over $600,000. Such can be the cost to the organization of informal group processes that have evolved into conflict.

While the examples given in the preceding pages by no means exhaust the infinite variety of informal processes that develop within organizations, they should provide some idea of the dual nature of organizations and a few of the consequences of a serious mismatch between purposes, structures, or processes of the formal and informal organizations. Table 1–2 summarizes the main points.

THE MANAGER'S ROLE IN THE ORGANIZATION

The basic responsibility of a manager is to see to it that the organization achieves its objectives. Typically, the manager coordinates the activities of others rather than performing operations himself or herself. While managers of smaller orga-

Table 1-2. The Dual Nature of Organizations

	Purpose	Structure	Process
The Formal Organization	Adequate financial return for effort, investment, and risk	Jobs, positions, organizational units; formal roles, relations, and rules; designated authority and accountability	Tasks, procedures, workflow sequences, formal organizational policies.
The Informal Organization	Satisfaction of personal, social, and psychological needs	Personal influence or power based on interpersonal and group skills, friendships, cliques, likes and dislikes, and ability to use job processes to advantage	Interpersonal processes, group processes, intergroup processes
Possible Consequences of Serious Mismatch	Low productivity, low profitability, may fail	Management and supervision have authority but lack power to make things happen the way they should and lack respect of workers. Low productivity, low profitability, may fail	Formal processes misused to satisfy personal needs. Production wasteful, inefficient; everything bogged down in red tape. Buckpassing, fingerpointing, game playing. Low productivity, low profitability, may fail

nizations may perform a number of operations (as does the gas station manager, who may pump gas, change tires, etc., as part of the job), these are not part of the role of manager. These additional duties merely reflect the fact that at times the management role does not require a full-time person. In this section we will be concerned only with the manager's role as manager, regardless of the amount of time actually spent doing something else.

Although hundreds of books have been written listing all the possible functions and responsibilities of managers, we will examine the manager's role in terms of four basic functions: (1) planning, (2) organizing, (3) leading, and (4) controlling. The manager may be involved in all of these activities more or less at the same time, or may concentrate on one or more for a time, depending on the organization's needs at the moment. The functions are highly interrelated and cannot successfully be performed independently. All four functions of the management role must be carefully integrated to produce an effective, smooth-running organization. In larger organizations, the manager may delegate much of the detail work associated with each function to staff assistants or subordinate managers. In small organizations he or she may personally perform all these functions. But in either case, the responsibility to see that they are performed, that they all fit together nicely, and that they are all consistent with the purpose, objectives, and goals of the organization is the manager's exclusively. The manager's skill in handling that responsibility is the key factor in the success of the organization. Let us examine briefly each of these four critical functions that constitute the essence of the managerial role.

Planning

In its simplest form, planning is *thinking ahead*, and as such is a vital part of any manager's role. It is also one of the most difficult things for a manager to do well. *Planning* means attempting to figure out ahead of time just what it is going to take to achieve an organizational objective or goal. Managers are responsible for many kinds of planning depending on the nature of the organization and their level in it. The primary planning efforts of managers at the lower levels of an organization are concerned with planning the work of their subordinates. The usual objective of such planning is to make sure that all the work gets done on time, without the use of overtime, without waste, and without overloading or underloading any individual. In other words, planning is concerned with making decisions about how best to use the organizational resources to meet objectives. There is always an element of uncertainty in any plan simply because no one can hope to anticipate *everything* before the activity has actually begun. As a consequence, the initial plan for any activity is merely the starting point. It will usually have to be readjusted periodically as the manager receives new information, as conditions change, or most important of all, as some initial assumptions prove to be incorrect. Planning therefore should be thought of as a process, a more or less continuous kind of activity for which a manager is responsible. As a process, it can be used by a manager to help build an effective team. By getting the people who must carry out the plans involved in the planning process, not only is the plan usually made much better, but also the chances of it being carried out are greatly improved. A team planning session helps everyone get a clear idea of exactly what the team objectives are and what must be done to reach them. *Each member has an opportunity to contribute his or her knowledge and experience to the plan. Equally important, all are more likely to be committed to the planned activity they had a say in developing.* The manager's role in the group planning process is to contribute his or her special knowledge and experience and to encourage all other members to contribute theirs. The manager also must provide guidelines so the first plan will not only achieve the objective, but also be acceptable to the larger organization of which the team may be a part. (For a full discussion of the managerial planning function see Brickner and Cope, *The Planning Process*, Winthrop Management Series.)

Organizing

Organizing and planning are closely related functions of the manager's role. Like planning, organizing may also be a more or less continuous process as conditions, objectives, product lines, and personnel change. To avoid confusing the two functions, we can think of *organizing* as actually putting together all the resources required to achieve some purpose. Resources include people, skills, time, money, equipment, and facilities. Planning usually precedes organizing, but planning a small business is obviously quite different from organizing a small business. The planning process may identify all of the work that has to be done, the order in which it must be done, and the schedule for completion of various tasks, but the organizing function involves actually assigning the various tasks to different people and coordinating their efforts. In other words, it amounts to actually developing the formal structure and formal processes of the organization. In performing this organizing function, the manager must always be mindful of the dual nature of organizations. She or he must not only organize resources to get the necessary work done, but must also try to build a social structure that helps meet the needs of people doing the work.

Leading

Good planning and good organizing can set the stage, but a manager must also provide active leadership if people are to work together to achieve organizational goals. Leadership involves the way a manager behaves in interpersonal relationships with subordinates. The leadership function is the activity that keeps the formal and informal organizations in tune. *Leading,* in other words, is striving to integrate the personal needs of the group members with the welfare of the organization. Perhaps the most important ingredients in leadership are enthusiasm for the work to be done; confidence in the intelligence and ability of the members to succeed; and the ability to influence the way people view their goals, their tasks, and their fellow workers. The effective leader knows that people have personal needs that they will try to satisfy while working in the organization. But at the same time the leader recognizes that cooperation and efficiency are necessary in order for the organization to achieve its goals at reasonable cost. Thus an important element in leadership is helping others see how they can satisfy some of their personal needs by satisfying the needs of the organization. Maintaining the balance between achievement of personal goals and achievement of organizational goals means that the manager, in leading, should know something about the individual, job-related needs of each team member. He or she must be willing to invest the time necessary to discuss what each hopes to get out of the group activity, then to try to find a way of enabling each to satisfy at least some of those needs without compromising the goals of the organization. When the manager in the leadership role operates in this way, he or she creates an atmosphere of trust, respect, openness, and confidence between himself or herself and subordinates.

True leadership is by no means all sweetness and light. There are times when a leader must be tough, must hold people to high performance standards, must discipline them or discharge them. However, by setting a good example, by creating a climate of openness, trust, and respect, by providing clear direction and a spirit of cooperation, the leader can minimize the situations which call for demonstrations of toughness.

Controlling

As one of the primary functions of management, *controlling* refers to the process of continually checking team progress toward the goal and making corrections when the team bogs down or the direction veers off the target. The manager must always know how the team is doing and how each individual is doing. If the manager has done a good job of organizing, planning, and leading, then controlling may be the easiest part of the job. In fact, the poorer job the manager does in performing the first three functions, the more difficulty he or she will have in controlling. Because controlling amounts to making sure the team is on time and on course, the importance of good planning and scheduling cannot be overstated. But to know how the team is progressing toward the common goal, and how each member is progressing on individual task goals, the manager must have some way of measuring performance and some way of getting feedback on performance from each member and from the group as a whole. It is not enough to wait until a task is due for completion to find out whether it will be done on time. To be of real help, the manager must know when team members are having serious difficulty or are not sure how best to proceed. Only then can he or she provide the help or guidance needed in time to save a lot of wasted effort and prevent needless frustration. The manager is most likely to receive the kind of continuous and spontaneous feedback needed if he or she has succeeded in creating a communication climate of openness, trust, and respect within the organization.

SUMMARY

This chapter provides an overview of the nature of an organization and the manager's role within the organization. To understand the manager's job, one must first understand the dual nature of an organization. A business consists of both a formal and informal organization. The formal organization is the official one described by organization charts, job descriptions, policy and procedure manuals, and work procedures.

Taken together, these documents describe how the whole organization is designed and intended to operate in order to achieve its formal purpose—usually to provide income for all participants in the enterprise. In addition to a formal purpose, the enterprise possesses a formal structure and formal processes. The structure of the formal organization can be defined in terms of the various job roles it designates, the relations among these roles, and the rules that are designed to keep people operating within their formal job roles. The formal processes of the enterprise describe the procedures to be followed by the various group members in order to make sure that their individual activities all fit together smoothly to accomplish the work of the organization.

The informal organization is the social system which inevitably emerges whenever a group of people spend much time working together. The purpose of the informal organization is to satisfy the personal social needs of the individual group members. The structure of the informal organization is based upon the likes, dislikes, friendships, animosities, and subgroups that develop as the individual group members attempt to satisfy some of their personal needs while doing their work. Of the many human needs that people attempt to satisfy in the working environment, three social needs seem to have the greatest effect on the formal organization: (1) the need for attention and approval; (2) the need to belong and conform; (3) the need to participate and contribute.

Informal processes emerge to support the developing informal structure as various group members find ways of using their positions to satisfy personal needs. Informal processes can occur at three different levels of interaction: (1) at the interpersonal level, where individuals attempt to redefine their formally assigned roles in a way that is more satisfying to their egos; (2) at the group level, where the members begin to pull together, or all head off in different directions; (3) at the intergroup level, where groups may either be in conflict or work together in friendly, productive cooperation. When members or groups do pull together, they may be helping the organization achieve its purpose or they may hinder the organization, depending on how well the purposes, structure, and processes of the formal and informal organization support each other, or match. One of the manager's responsibilities is to influence the development of the informal organization in the pursuit of the organization's goals.

The cardinal responsibility of a manager is to see to it that the organization achieves its objectives. The basic functions of the manager's job include planning, organizing, leading, and controlling. In large organizations managers may delegate much of the detail associated with these functions to staff assistants or subordinate managers. In small organizations the manager may personally perform all of these activities. In either case, he or she has the responsibility to see that they are performed, that they are well integrated, and that they are consistent with the purpose, objectives, and goals of the organization.

Planning is thinking ahead to figure out just what will be required to achieve an organizational objective or goal. It is concerned with making decisions about how best to use organizational resources to meet objectives. Usually plans must be frequently modified as conditions change or new information becomes available.

Organizing is the activity of actually putting together all of the resources required to achieve some purpose. Resources include people, skills, time, money, equipment, and facilities. Organizing involves assigning the various tasks to different people and coordinating their efforts. Like the planning function, the manager often finds that organizing is an ongoing activity that requires frequent attention, especially as plans change.

Leadership is the function that keeps the formal and informal organizations in tune. It involves the way a manager behaves in interpersonal relationships with subordinates and strives to integrate the personal needs of the group members with the needs of the organization. One of the most powerful tools available to the leader for influencing the behavior of team members and creating a high-performance climate is the example set by his or her own behavior.

Controlling is the management function of continually checking team progress toward the goal and making corrections when the team bogs down or veers off course. To do a good job of controlling, the manager must have some way of measuring performance and some way of getting feedback on performance from each member and from the group as a whole. If the manager performs planning, organizing, and leading functions well, controlling may be the easiest part of the job.

ASSIGNMENTS

1. Organize the class into groups of about six members each.
2. Each group selects a small business such as a gas station, restaurant, movie theater, florist shop, drugstore, clothing store, or any small business with a manager or manager/owner that has at least two employees.
3. Contact the manager for permission to spend some time talking with him or her and the company's employees and observing them as they go about their work.
4. Organize your group to carry out the following specific assignments:
    a. Identify and write up the formal purpose of the business.
    b. Identify and describe in writing the formal structure of the business.

   c. Identify and describe the formal processes of the business.

   d. Identify and write up the informal purposes of the organization.

   e. Identify and describe the informal structure of the organization.

   f. Identify and describe the informal processes of the organization.

5. Working as a project team, plan, organize, prepare, and present to the rest of the class an oral report complete with visual aids. Special attention should be given to evaluating whether the formal and informal organizations are well matched or appear to be mismatched. In either case, present your evaluation of the effects of the match or mismatch on the success of the business.

REFERENCES

BRICKNER, WILLIAM, AND COPE, DONALD. *The Planning Process.* Cambridge, Mass.: Winthrop Publishers, 1977.

JAMES, MURIEL, AND JONGEWARD, DOROTHY. *Born to Win.* Menlo Park, Ca.: Addison-Wesley, 1971.

LEAVITT, H. J. *Managerial Psychology.* Chicago: University of Chicago Press, 1964.

RUSH, H. M. F. *Behavioral Science: Concepts and Management Application.* New York: The National Industrial Conference Board, 1969.

SHOMPER, RICHARD F., AND PHILLIPS, VICTOR F., JR. *Management in Bureaucracy.* New York: AMACOM, 1973.

PANEL DISCUSSION

Panelists

Shirley R. Chilton, M.B.A., Chairman of the Board, Daniel Reeves and Company, Inc. She has over twenty years' experience in the brokerage business, from switchboard operator to registered representative to board manager to chief executive officer. She has lectured and co-authored texts introducing economic principles to elementary-school students for which she has won two Freedom Foundation awards. Currently she is completing a doctorate degree at the U.S.C. Graduate School of Management.

Robert A. Covington, M.P.A., Chief Administrative Officer, San Bernardino County, California, since 1959. He has had management experience in both the public and private sectors. He has been instrumental in organizing and restructuring government agencies to achieve efficiency and to assure the greatest contributions from and satisfaction for each employee.

Earl J. Ends, Ph.D., Professor of Behavioral Science, Pepperdine University, School of Business and Management. He has held a variety of professional and management positions in both private and public organizations over the past twenty years. His major interests and his consulting practice center around management selection, management development, and organization development.

David T. Farrell, B.S., Director of Employee Relations, James B. Lansing Sound Inc. He has taken additional graduate work, at the Loyola Law School and the U.C.L.A. Graduate School of Management, in industrial relations and behavioral sciences. He has over twenty-five years experience in full-service personnel and industrial relations positions, with recent interest in and emphasis on "Quality of Working Life" programs for employees at J. B. Lansing Sound Inc.

Walter J. Kruel, M.B.A., Corporate Vice President, Corporate Development and Planning, Lear Siegler Inc. He has over twenty years' experience in plant management as chief executive officer and group executive, and he is a member of numerous industry associations and The World Future Society.

Curtis W. Page, Ph.D., Professor of Behavior Science. He previously served as Associate Dean in Pepperdine University's School of Business and Management. He is also president of his own consulting firm, The Page Group, Inc. His twenty-one years' experience includes actively consulting, teaching, and managing in both large and small public- and private-sector organizations. His major interests have centered around group dynamics, organizational development, and stimulating individuals and groups toward optimal productivity and satisfaction.

Discussion

Page: Dave, will you please give us your opening statement on Chapter 1, on the organization and the manager's role in the organization?

Farrell: Since I don't have a substantial academic background in this field, I decided I would start my investigation by using no less of an authority than Webster to define some of the terms. Interestingly enough, I looked up the term *team* first and came up with the definition that I thought would set the tone for this meeting. Webster's primary definition of *team* is, "a line of animals harnessed together." (Laughter)

Webster calls *organization* "the state of being organized," so I went to *organize* and found it was "to arrange or constitute in interdependent parts, each having a special function or relation with respect to the whole." My intention in this part was really to express a number of points of view. There is a lot of material to cover and I decided to express some random thoughts that occurred to me as I was reading the

Earl J. Ends

L to R: Ends, Chilton, Farrell, and Covington

Curtis W. Page

L to R: Covington, Page, Ends, Chilton, and Kruel

L to R: Ends, Chilton, and Kruel

material. On the nature of the organization, I did notice that the concept of organizations having *principles* and *values* wasn't expressed in the material. I want to emphasize the "principle" aspects first. It has been my experience more often than not that principles and values tend not to be stated in an explicit way. Rarely do I see them committed to writing as a *statement* of principles and values of the organization. But nonetheless they do exist, and if not stated are the sum total and aggregate of the principles and values of the members within the organization. Whether stated or unstated, they influence the activities of the organization. It would seem beneficial for a clear sense of identity for an organization to have that kind of statement.

Also, I thought about the relationship between the organization's overall *goals and objectives* and its *humanness* . . . questions about whether the leaders in an organization consider those two aspects to be in harmony or conflicting. To what extent do they see the humanness of the organization to be a fact of life and therefore recognized?

Focusing next on the functions of a manager, I have from time to time thought of a manager as an architect, using that term in the sense of a creator of an environment or space in which some good things can happen. In that context, the most appropriate use of resources, materials, and the human resources should be one that is in harmony with their own nature rather than trying to force them to serve only the needs of the organization. Also from time to time managers are viewed as having a role that is not dissimilar from that of the parent in terms of primary responsibilities for training and development.

On the subject of planning, I kept thinking as I was reading that one fundamental mistake that managers may make in the field of planning is carrying it too far. What the manager should really be planning is his own job and his own responsibilities—but how easy it is for a manager to just continue in such a detailed way that he ends up leaving little space for his subordinates to do any planning of their own work. It seems to me that may happen, first of all, as a function of an individual manager's needs for control and also as a function of his assumptions about other people. If he assumes his subordinates are incompetent or not to be trusted, he is likely to decide he had better do all of the planning himself.

On "feedback." I feel the *timeliness* of feedback is exceedingly important. If a mother tried to give a five-year-old child annual performance appraisals, how well would that work in terms of training development? Also, feedback need not come unilaterally from the manager or supervisor, but he should look for opportunities to build relationships into an organization so that feedback is direct, immediate, and comes from a variety of sources. In many cases, that direct feedback would be less judgmental about the overall person. It doesn't cast the supervisor as much in the role of a judge of another person's total being. Many times the work can be designed so that a person can get direct and immediate feedback when a mistake occurs, either directly from the work itself or from peers within the organization.

Page: Dave, you commented on many aspects of points made in the chapter. You added some things that seemed to me to be essential characteristics of an organization. A major concept you added was that, indeed, there are "values" involved. We talked of purpose, and, just as you pointed out, many times the values are implicit and not stated with reference to the purpose of the organization. What do you others think?

Chilton: In identifying the place to begin in establishing an organization I have always found that it is important to sit back and ask, "What kind of environment are we working in?" and to have a perception of how each individual fits into that environment—knowing as much as you can about their backgrounds—How they got where they are, how they perceive themselves where they are. And one approach that I have always taken, having started out in sales, is—"know your customer." And that means know your environment and know the individuals within the environment. How are you going to put them together to maximize your goals and objectives? It is extremely important to structure action so that people are utilizing their talents and time, because when they have too much time on their hands they find that they are not proud of what they are accomplishing. They have to be moving and when you set the example and the tone, you'll get twice as much done. That's why I consider identifying the environment and the people working in that environment the first stage of developing an organization.

Farrell: Of course, we must know the business environment in which we are operating—its economics, relationships with shareholders (if there are shareholders), or relationships with the public. It is important to understand and be responsive to and know what the priorities are and to tie those back to our values. To what extent are we going to make the stockholders happy and at the same time be concerned with personal development within the organization? To what extent are these purposes in harmony or conflict?

Kruel: Most business organizations promote the belief that their one single identifiable goal is to attract business and provide return to their stockholders. This goal, at least in concept, is correct because keeping the stockholders happy generally provides continuity to the organization.

However, the ones to benefit most from stockholder happiness are the management on the top of the organization, because they are personally rewarded by and voted into power by stockholders. Therefore one can conclude that stockholder happiness is beneficial and necessary because it provides rewards, or satisfies what top management wants or expects from the organization. Further downward in the organization the stockholder becomes less meaningful because his value to the organization becomes less recognizable. The stockholder is less important in directly satisfying the needs of the lower levels of the organization.

With the potential that there exists a great variety of job satisfaction needs on the part of organization team members, the job of management in the personal development role becomes one of extremely high priority.

I believe that the successful organizations recognize that people within the organization do not really see themselves as working to satisfy the stockholders. They see themselves as working to satisfy the things they want and need from the organization. Leadership bridges the needs of the stockholders and the needs of the individuals within the framework of the organization, trying to find the happy compromise where everyone can obtain everything they would like to have.

Covington: Also, if you achieve what you are pointing to, you not only help the individual employee, but you help the goal of the stockholder as well, because the individual will produce. If he is satisfied, he will produce more effectively and, in turn, that is going to reflect on your profit sheet.

Kruel: I see it as very interrelated, it's a cycle and it's continuous.

Farrell: I wonder how much of a reflection that is of most managements' points of view? That's the question: To what extent do most managements see those goals as harmonious and interdependent?

Chilton: I see this as one of the main thrusts and purposes of this type of book. If we do *not* strengthen the values and principles of ethical business and the attitudes toward the humanizing of work in the corporate structure, business will succumb to the ravages of ever-increasing government control.

Page: Would you just say business? Or would you say public sector as well as private sector organizations?

Chilton: Every type of operation or organization. It's a cultural revolution that we are experiencing. I think it is prompted primarily by the development and extension of communication. Everybody knows what's going on with everyone and therefore they either want to participate and have part of the action or to understand it at least.

Page: Perhaps we could think of two different kinds of organizations: (1) The Frederick Taylor–Max Weber, obviously typically bureaucratic kind of structure, and (2) the Argyris-

Herzberg–Davis (and a host of others), sociotechnical, highly participative organization.

Covington: That would recognize two extremes. One a highly participative approach and the other the traditional, conservative approach of a few years ago. I really think there have been a lot of changes. But personally I can't go to either of the extremes although I've come from the Taylor extreme, in my exposure. I've run the gamut, and I believe there is a middle ground where there still have to be some activities that are in some way autocratic and dictatorial. At the same time, I know that today we are permitting input. We are encouraging the subordinate supervisors, and even the employees, to participate in management decisions that wouldn't even have been considered twenty or thirty years ago. I think input is important, and the opportunity for input by the individual in the organization, regardless of his status, helps make a better organization. At the same time, the final decision must be made by the top management.

Chilton: I don't think that what I was relating to was necessarily participation by the employees in management decisions. I think the integration of planning and procedures should include input from whomever is involved.

Covington: Aren't those management decisions?

Chilton: Yes, but what I meant primarily was that goals of the organization should encompass the entire community—working and social. The responsibility to the community, I think, was mentioned. How many organizations have this type of goal in mind in the structure of their objectives as opposed to only satisfying the stockholders? Business depends on a healthy community, and vice versa. The question of satisfying the community's social needs is a responsibility and it belongs to everyone.

With reference to who makes the decision, I believe the term "autocratic decision" is another name for many "executive decisions," which we all have to make. Ultimately the buck stops here.

Page: I would think that "autocratic decision" has another connotation, which is more of a connotation of "unilateral, without participation."

It seems to me the Frederick Taylor–Max Weber, highly bureaucratic model implies certain kinds of values. It implies values that people have. It makes assumptions about the nature of people and the trustworthiness of people. And indeed the participative model implies values and assumptions about people. That's what I was getting at.

Farrell: As you well know, that point of view is at the heart of what we are doing in our company.

Page: That could be interesting if you would tell us something about it, Dave.

Farrell: About a year ago we began studying ways in which we might modify the typical hierarchical structure of decision making, extend employee participation in decisions, and so forth. We have begun the actual work on that just about six weeks ago, so I can't say much about results yet. We have put together a planning council, with the majority of participants being nonmanagement employees. Most of them were brought to that position through election by their peers, and the charter of that planning council is extremely broad. We talked for many, many months in the planning stage about the issue of expectations, and should we define the parameters and limits of decision-making authority of that group in advance, and that kind of thing. With some trepidation, we opted not to. That group is meeting without specific limitations at this point, except that until it is agreed that ways of operating are changed, we will continue to operate in the old way, so that we are not all of a sudden creating chaos. We have begun to brainstorm things that can be done and there has been some emphasis given to looking at the nature and content of the work, feeling that that is an essential ingredient to making work more enriching and satisfying. Following the basic principle of participation, we have a number of task forces working now in various departments within the company. Their task is to seek ways in which decision making in the work group can be continually expanded. We haven't precluded the possibility that the decisions made typically by management could ultimately be made by that group or by the workers themselves.

Covington: Does that group include supervisors as well?

Farrell: Yes. The planning council has twelve people on it; seven of them are nonsupervisory employees, two are supervisory employees elected by their peer supervisors, and three are supervisors appointed by the president of the company. There is no one theory nor one principle from which our effort comes. We, in looking at all the possibilities, decided not to merely transfer a theory or an experiment or something that was done elsewhere into our situation. We are just going to let it grow out of our own particular unique set of environmental conditions.

Page: Could we move on in this discussion as you think about this model that Dave has just described versus the models you have in your thinking? Can you move on into planning, organizing, leading, and controlling, with reference to the manager's role in whatever kind of an organization you may be thinking of? I guess the question is: How do you utilize the planning function? What do you include and how do you go about it?

Kruel: The planning history that I have observed has been most interesting in its evolution. The organization started as a small company with about $12 million in annual sales. The basic business was bought by a group of investors as a nucleus for building a large firm. From that start, they continued to buy, merge, and acquire other firms until they reached annual sales volume of about $650 million. There was a goal and a basic plan in the minds of a few people during this development. I think this was an illustration of "opportunity planning". As acquisitions occurred our stock value increased and we could trade stock for more companies—all the result of very informal planning. One day we paused in the midst of these activities and realized that we had a very sizable organization, and somebody said, "We must plan." I think that the real issue here was a feeling that we had to formally plan rather than let everything be so opportunistic or random in its development.

My experience in planning has provoked an interesting question concerning planning that is generally avoided by most organizations. That question is: For what are we planning?

We went from a very informal "Why plan?" system to a procedure that was very much participative, one which must be defined as "bottoms up". That system was one based on using the inputs of as many employees as possible—within the limits of their ability to handle the issues of planning and our ability to handle the number of issues—in order to develop the foundation for the plan. In some divisions everyone participated and in many other divisions only 10 or 20 percent of the employees were involved. The system is based on each participant writing his thoughts as they relate to the business on a piece of paper, identifying those things that he felt were good as being strengths, and identifying those unsatisfactory items as either faults or threats to the business. The format called for them to identify what the specific issue was that they were drawing, why they felt that way, and what they would do to either rectify a problem or take advantage of an opportunity, if it was their decision to make. Each idea or issue was written on a separate piece of paper. Each issue was received by the management of the business entity and was recognized as the personal input of one of their employees. We never allowed them to discard any of the issues even if it was felt that it was not germane to the planning process. Each one of these pieces of paper was folded into a grouping that we called "action programs". The management group of the division would sort the issues and categorize them by the functional area with which they dealt. We would finally end up with a reasonable number of action items which called for specific things to be done during the coming months or years. These action items usually would be based on eight or ten of the planning issues, and we would have ten, twenty, or even forty of these actions in the plan of that division. This system satisfied the need for a formal planning system because, in fact, we had a system with rules drawn up and a procedure for building a plan and carrying out the actions. It also satisfied the need for participation among the employees because everyone had an opportunity to make an input into the plan. They felt they had some impact on the future of the company and on their own personal future.

From the standpoint of satisfying top management of the corporation, we found that the system failed in its primary function of giving the company a direction. We found that top management was more in a position of having to listen to the consensus of a lot of people's views rather than contributing and participating themselves. This, of course, was bad in that the top management had skills and an overview of the corporation which was much greater than that of the people at the grass-roots level. People with the best qualifications and, in fact, with the responsibility for planning the course of the future, didn't have an equal vote in the system. It was a great system for the employees and for middle and lower levels of management, but top corporate management's input was minimized in the process. This was very disturbing to our top management and provoked the question, "For what are we planning?"

Farrell: They had more facts, certainly.

Kruel: Well, it was interesting that the facts we received generally dealt with personal issues, the concerns that involved the contributing individuals, more than they involved the issues of the company. This was natural because often the participants were not fully aware of the overall company needs. We did have a lot of personal satisfaction there, but we didn't achieve much in terms of satisfying and recognizing overall company needs.

In trying to re-establish something that made more sense, we wanted to have individual participation, but also, more important, we needed attention to the overall direction, especially since national and world-wide economics were changing. We didn't have as much economic freedom to do as many things as we had, say, ten years ago. The approach we use developed from six basic corporate objectives which are very broad, extremely ideal, and which would fit any company in the world. In attempting to integrate our planning system into those objectives we found that *definition* was a basic problem. Everybody was using words, but the words didn't mean the same thing to everybody. We had fifty-odd divisions with hundreds of people using words like objectives, goals, strategies, tactics, and so on, but each meant something different to everyone. So our first campaign was to identify what we thought the words should mean, and why, and to communicate what our common definitions were till we were all talking the same language.

Page: When you say "your first campaign or thrust," was that you personally or through your managers?

Kruel: Through managers discussing what the terms or definitions meant and what they should mean, and recognizing that we should also be flexible to people's needs and accept changes in our planning language if those changes made the system more palatable and in turn more usable. The point being that, through open discussion exchange, we developed our planning vocabulary, and from that developed a language which everybody would find acceptable and understandable because they participated in the definition. The planning system today does have participation of the individual. Standardization of information is necessary, as is standardization of language, because many different entities supplying information in different forms generally want to maintain a separate identity. We satisfied that by having participating conferences for identifying what that format should be. The ideal system has a "bottom-up" planning ingredient with modifications by a "top-down" input or adjustment. The *market/business audit* is a term which is a summary of thoughts regarding the market and business aspects of a product line. The market/business audit is a jogger to evaluate all aspects of product management, including technical aspects, the marketing aspects, the organizational aspect, personnel, etc. The market/business audit is further modified to include higher-level inputs by the use of what we call "corporate group priorities." The point being that, from an overall company standpoint, we have some overall priority needs to be communicated to divisions because they could be working off in an entirely different direction based on their needs or desires alone. This is essentially a negotiating session between the division priorities and the corporate priorities. It is very difficult to have severe differences with the corporate directions because those are fundamental and governed by corporate economics. The goals are then defined as things at which we direct ourselves during the year. These are then backed by strategies on how to achieve gains, and tactics, which are really "action items". Each goal can have many strategies, and each strategy can have many tactics. So it is very important to have a good definition and identification of goals or objectives. We then have a pyramid of strategies, beneath which is a pyramid of tactics. The tactics should include things such as money, people, place, dates, that type of thing. One other function is one to follow up on tactics, which we call "tactical assessment". Tactical assessment is a method of continually feeding back through the year with the line management and also with the participating committee. An update is held to review planning; this is an easy way of opening the door for all sorts of discussions. An update on the planning sometimes leads to changes on the basic tactics. But this system seems to work well because lower-level participants and top management people feel that their inputs are there—they're committed to it. Line management is committed also because they have been involved in putting the plan together along with other people in the divisional organization.

two

The Manager's Role as Team Leader

OBJECTIVES

After reading Chapter Two you should be able to:

1. Identify a specific set of learnable activities and skills that make up the managerial leadership role.
2. Describe several different ways a manager can influence the behavior of others.
3. Discuss how one approaches the task of acquiring basic management skills.

INTRODUCTION

Leadership is only one of the elements of the overall job of being a manager, but it is a very vital one. In this chapter we will first explore the managerial leadership function in more detail, then we will look at the key managerial skill: influencing others. Finally we will consider how one might go about developing the basic skills of management.

WHAT IS LEADERSHIP?

Simply stated, *leadership* is the ability to influence the thinking, the attitudes, and the behavior of subordinates in some desired direction. While the *behavior* of subordinates can often be influenced in the desired direction by use of pressure, force, and punishment, such tactics usually cause their thinking and their attitudes to move in an undesirable direction. In such situations, the manager is using coercion, not leadership. A key ingredient in leadership is that subordinates *willingly allow* the leader to influence not only their behavior, but also their thinking and their attitudes. In order for subordinates to allow this to occur, the leader must somehow capture their imaginations in a way that helps them see that by willingly striving to attain organization objectives they will also satisfy some of their personal needs, such as self-esteem, esteem from others, a sense of competence, a feeling of belonging, a feeling of personal significance, and a feeling of growth. While this may seem like magic, or perhaps a special talent that only the chosen few are born with, such is not the case. Leadership is a skill, and all skills are learnable.

Perhaps the best way to take some of the mystery out of leadership is to regard it as simply one kind of role that managers often have to take, then to break the role behaviors down into the various functions or specific behaviors that make up the role of leader. It should be kept in mind that it is not necessary for a team leader to perform all of these functions alone. The leader's responsibility is to make sure that each of the functions discussed below are performed well enough by one or more group members (including the manager) so the team objectives will be met. The leader must be prepared to personally perform these functions until team members develop the skill and initiative to share in the leadership functions.

BASIC FUNCTIONS OF THE LEADERSHIP ROLE

In the leadership role, the manager, if he or she hopes to develop a high-performance team, must be sure that all the following functions are performed. It should be noted that all of the functions involve *interaction* with the team members individually or as a group.

Establish, Communicate, and Clarify the Goals

The importance of clearly formulated goals cannot be overestimated. Not only must the goals be crystal clear in the leader's mind, but also they must be equally clear in the minds of all the team members. Every team member must know exactly what the team is attempting to accomplish in terms as specific as possible. For example, a goal stated in general terms, such as "raise some money to buy athletic equipment for the school," can mean a dozen different things to a dozen different people. To one person it may mean only several hundred dollars for new basketballs, to another it may mean several thousand dollars for additional gymnastic equipment. *When stated goals are nonspecific it is virtually impossible to develop plans to achieve them and absolutely impossible to secure genuine commitment from group members.* Without specific goals, group members have no way of estimating how much time and effort will be expected of them, whether the plans are realistic, or even whether they are interested in participating. Further, it is not enough for the leader to clearly understand the specific goals. He or she must make sure that each team member understands with equal clarity. This may require considerable group discussion time, but it is well worth whatever time is required.

Secure Commitment to the Goals

Commitment to a goal means that an individual finds a specific goal desirable enough so that he or she is willing to invest some time, energy, and abilities to help achieve it. It is important enough so that the individual is willing to juggle current priorities to make room for the new activity. Since most people manage to fill their waking hours with some kind of activity, new activities usually mean giving up or reducing time devoted to current activities. Thus the first question in the minds of prospective team members usually is: What's in it for me? The second question is: Is the payoff worth the effort required of me and worth what I have to give up in order to receive the payoff? Unless these questions are satisfactorily answered in the mind of each prospective team member, there will be little or no genuine commitment to the goal.

Securing commitment to team goals is one of the leader's most difficult, but also one of the most vital, tasks. If the leader neglects this function, the best that person can hope for is uninspired, mediocre performance from the group.

Define and Negotiate Roles

The part each member will play in the team effort must be clearly defined and negotiated with the various members. This amounts to securing agreement on how the group will organize to achieve its goals; defining the structure of the organization. At a minimum, the roles, the relations between them, and basic ground rules for interaction must be identified and agreed on by the group members. Usually role assignments will tend to be based upon possession of needed skill, talent, experience, and interest in taking the role. Negotiation is often necessary to make sure that everything required by a role actually is accepted as part of the assignment. Otherwise only the fun part of the job may get done. For example, a member may enjoy initial sales contacts, but hate the follow-up contacts or the paperwork required and thus neglect those tasks. Therefore, while he or she may be very active, this individual may contribute very little toward the goals of the organization. The person who accepts the role must be willing to take the bitter with the sweet, and must be willing to accept responsibility for the whole task.

Secure Commitment to the Roles Assigned

Just as with the team goals, all members must be committed to fulfilling their assigned roles to the best of their ability. This is more likely to happen if each member has had some say in defining roles and has had the opportunity to negotiate the specifics to more nearly match the role he or she had hoped to play. If a team member is initially committed to the team goal, but is unhappy with the role assigned, he or she will usually lose commitment to the team goal. The reason is clear: When one decides that there is not much self-reward in a task, one loses interest in the group effort.

Plan the Activity and Make It Clear

When the activities of the various team members must be coordinated to achieve team objectives, some kind of planning is required for even simple activities. While participative planning involving all group members has many advantages, it is the leader's responsibility to make sure the plan is a good one. It is also the team leader's responsibility to make sure that each member really understands the part of the plan that member is responsible for, how it fits into the overall team effort, and the importance of the schedule for various aspects of the effort.

Set Performance Standards and Make Sure
They Are Understood

Leaders of high-performing, high-morale groups typically have higher performance standards for the team than do the individual members. But such standards have the desired positive effect on performance and morale only if they are clearly communicated. In doing so, the leader is telling the team exactly what is expected of them, how good he expects them to be as individual performers, and how good he expects them to be as a team. While leaders' standards must be within reason, they should be high enough so everyone has to stretch to achieve them. By doing this, the leader is offering both a challenge and an opportunity to each person to discover and to demonstrate that he or she is capable of better performance than ever achieved before.

Provide Feedback to Individuals and to the Group

Feedback is vital for two reasons. First it prevents wasted effort, time, and resources when tasks are not being performed as required. Second it provides evidence of progress toward the goal when tasks are being performed correctly, and therefore provides recognition of satisfactory effort. When appropriate, favorable feedback to the effect that a team member is doing well on an assigned task amounts to a positive stroke. Feedback on group performance as a whole is equally important and beneficial. It makes the members begin to feel that they are on a winning team, which begins to increase enthusiasm for the effort and increases morale.

Provide Coaching and/or Supervision

A very important function of the leader is to make sure that every team member gets the coaching and supervision that he or she needs to perform at the level the standards require. This not only continually reinforces the standards, but also helps each person develop competence in the task at hand. It also reaffirms the importance of each member's performance to the team effort, and makes members feel like others are interested in helping them succeed as individuals.

Provide Initiative, Enthusiasm, and a Sense
of Purpose, and Set an Example

The leader serves as an example for the team members. As a consequence, the leader's own behavior tends to set the behavior norms for the group. If the leader wants team members to be enthusiastic, he or she must be enthusiastic. If the leader wants them to show initiative, he or she must display initiative. If the leader wants them to be open and honest in dealing with each other, he or she must be open and honest in interpersonal relations. In brief, the leader must model the behavior and attitudes he or she wants team members to adopt.

Control the Climate and the Group Process

The *climate* of a group refers to how the team members feel about one another, how much they enjoy working together, and how they feel about their joint endeavor. It is a mix of attitudes, emotions, and interpersonal behavior. The leader can control the climate first by example and second by dealing directly with inappropriate attitudes, feelings, and behavior on the part of individual team members. For example, if a team member becomes discouraged with his or her own progress, the leader must deal with the discouragement before it poisons the whole team.

The group *process* refers to how the team members interact or work together to achieve the team goals. As a general rule, group process and group climate are two sides of the same coin. They are highly interdependent. They are also highly dependent on the extent to which the leader has ensured that the other functions of leadership are being performed.

In summary, it is the responsibility of the manager in the leadership role to ensure that all the management functions are performed. It is not necessary that the manager personally perform all of them. In fact, sharing leadership functions is the typical mode of operation in high-performing groups. It encourages much greater involvement of the individual team members and is much more rewarding for them.

THE KEY SKILL: INFLUENCING OTHERS

The key skill in learning to become an effective manager is skill in influencing others. To develop a high-performing team the manager must be able to influence not only the overt behavior of team members, but also their thinking, their attitudes, and even some of their feelings. The manager must be able to influence others' total behavior for the good of the organization. The ability to influence others in this way is the basis of power in any organization. In fact, *power* and *the ability to influence the behavior of others* are interchangeable terms. However, power can be exercised autocratically or democratically. McClelland and Burnham have found that the manager who exercises power in an autocratic style generally makes people feel weak and powerless. On the other hand, the manager who uses the democratic or coaching style will generally have subordinates who feel strong and responsible and who have high team spirit. Since the ability to influence others is a learnable skill, let us examine this skill more closely. We will discuss influence under four headings. First we will look at influencing the individual. Second we will explore influencing a small group. Third we will discuss group development. Finally we will examine the interaction influence principle.

Influencing Individuals

Influencing people one at a time, on a one-to-one basis, is a distinctly different skill from influencing a group of people as a group. Many people who feel quite comfortable leading group activities feel quite uncomfortable dealing with people on a one-to-one basis, and vice versa. To become a truly effective manager or team leader, one must develop both skills. In some ways, influencing people one at a time is a more difficult skill to learn. It is difficult and perhaps even threatening to some because neither the team member nor the team leader can rely on the group for support. One is on one's own in the interaction. Then, too, in one-to-one interactions feelings tend to be much more evident and tend to play a larger part in the outcome. The physical closeness and the relatively undivided attention given to the participants make it difficult to hide or disguise true feelings. Even if the precise feeling is hidden, the other person usually senses that something is being hidden. In other words, one feels that the other person is not leveling. This puts a person on guard and the communication channel between the two is apt to become cluttered with so much noise that the possibility of constructive influence vanishes. How can this be prevented?

The essence of a good one-to-one relationship is mutual trust. It is a relationship in which neither party feels a need to keep defenses up. It is a relationship in which both parties are open, honest, and respectful. This creates a feeling of rapport which establishes communication and keeps the channel open for constructive influence. It is not enough that the team leader *intends* to be constructive; the team members must *feel* that the leader *is* being constructive. But what does that mean? Generally it means that the team members feel and believe that the manager is sincerely interested in helping them support or enhance their self-images. Thus a good manager or team leader is one who is interested in and able to help people perform better than they could on their own. The relationship that satisfies these requirements is often referred to as the *coaching relationship.*

The Coaching Relationship

The coaching relationship begins with two convictions on the part of the person taking the role of the coach. The first conviction is that the team member wants to perform better and is capable of performing better, and that the only reason he or she is not doing better is because he or she does not know how. The second conviction, which must be shared by the team member as well, is that the coach will be able to help the team member learn how to improve performance. As was the case with leadership functions, the team leader does not necessarily have to personally provide all the coaching that various team members may require. The leader's responsibility is to see to it that necessary coaching is provided by someone and that it has the desired effect. *The important point to note here is that coaching is one of the most powerful tools available to the manager for influencing individual team members.*

The Coaching Process

The team leader in most cases is concerned with on-the-job coaching. In other words, coaching efforts are aimed at helping various individuals close the gap between some current skill level or level of performance and that level required by the job that must be done. This means that the coach must have a pretty clear idea of the level of performance actually required in order to make a success of the team effort. Above all, the leader must be realistic in setting performance standards and performance-improvement standards. Expecting or demanding perfection when it is not required by the job is a sure way to turn subordinates off. Expecting or demanding too rapid an improvement will have the same effect. As a consequence, one of the coach's important responsibilities is that of setting objectives for the person to be coached. The objectives must be clearly defined, perfectly understood, and accepted by both the coach and the learner. This is more likely to occur when both have had a hand in setting the objectives. The reason for this is obvious: If the learner feels no need to improve, or has no desire to improve, then he or she is not likely to accept the performance standards the coach believes are necessary. If the learner does not accept the coach's objectives, he or she will not try to reach them. Thus one of the advantages of the joint setting of performance or performance-improvement objectives is that it gives both coach and learner an opportunity to discuss the learner's current performance and the requirements of the position from both points of view. Usually, in joint goal setting, the coach is trying to determine how much improvement is realistic for the learner and how much of a commitment to improving performance the learner is willing to make, while the learner is looking for reassurance from the coach that he or she is capable of improving and is wondering how much actual help to expect from the coach.

Once the performance goal or objective is agreed on, a plan is made for carrying it out. The plan consists of an agreement regarding how and when the learner will get an opportunity to learn and practice and how much help will be given by the coach. If the performance required is something the learner has never done before, the coach really has two roles: that of teacher first and coach second. In the teaching role the leader makes sure the learner understands what is involved in the basic task and shows the learner how the job is done, perhaps several times. Then the leader asks the learner to perform the task several times to make sure the learner can perform all the elements of the task without getting mixed up, leaving things out, or making too many errors, thus indicating the learner has reached some minimum level of skill.

If higher performance is required, then more coaching is required. Remember, the aim of coaching is to improve performance or to increase skill levels. *The distinction between learning how to do something and developing skill at doing it is important, especially from the manager's viewpoint.* The manager can often delegate the teaching task to another team member to conserve the manager's time for coaching after the learner has mastered the basic elements of the job. An example may help to illustrate the point.

One of the large airlines employs a number of passenger service agents who must, among other duties, answer telephone inquiries about flight schedules, ticket prices, and itineraries. This contact with the public provides a natural opportunity for sales promotion of the company's services. The company training department has developed a program to teach the trainees the basic ingredients of the job. Such things as the proper way to answer the phone, how to use the timetables, how to calculate the fares, and how to help select the best routes are covered. Since many callers have not decided which airline they want to take or even exactly when and if they will take a trip, the agent has an opportunity to sell the caller on using the airline in question rather than some other. While suggested ways to perform the sales part of the job were included in the training program—including specific phrases to use—management felt that few of these potential customers were actually being sold on using the airline's services. After discussion with supervisors and agents, the training department realized that much of the passenger agent's job was a matter of knowledge, not skill, and could be learned more or less mechanically in a classroom. The sales function, however, was not a matter of knowledge only, but was more than anything else a matter of skill. Skills are learned by doing, and proficiency is developed by practice and coaching. While initially most of the passenger agents used the phrases they had learned in the training program, they were often used mechanically and seldom resulted in convincing a caller to order a ticket if the caller's mind was not already made up. Due to lack of success, the typical passenger agent soon quit using the selling phrases he or she had learned and began to believe that selling was not really an important part of the job anyway.

The problem was solved by a program that began with group discussions with the passenger agents stressing the importance of the sales function of their jobs to the well being of the airline. (They operated in a highly competitive market and were not maintaining their share of the market.) Once the passenger agents were convinced of the importance and the desirability of increased sales on their part, the next step was to secure from each passenger agent a commitment to try to improve individual sales performance. The passenger agents felt that, while they understood the general mechanics of selling, they did not have the skill to apply their knowledge to actually close a sale. They felt they needed some special help. To deal with this felt need, the training department devised an on-the-job coaching program. Each passenger agent agreed to try to make as many sales as possible for a two-week period, using whatever sales skill and knowledge he or she could muster. Records were kept so the agents could see just how well they were doing on their own and could compare results with those of fellow workers. This step of the program accomplished three things. First, it succeeded in getting all of the passenger agents to really try to sell and to think about how they might improve their performance. Second, it provided a base line from which to establish performance-improvement goals and from which to measure progress. Third, it enabled the coaches to diagnose each person's performance and begin to formulate plans for improvement. Sales were up during the two-week period simply because everybody was really trying. These results convinced the agents that they actually could influence sales and so they became interested in learning how to become more effective telephone sellers. In other words, they had done as well as they could on their own, now they were ready for coaching. Coaching was initially performed by several consultants who spent some time with each agent helping diagnose problems in sales techniques. This included a discussion of what the agent seemed to be doing well, what the agent was doing poorly, and what he or she was not doing at all. The coach and the agent agreed on an improvement plan that outlined which type of sales situation or customer the agent needed the most help with. Since agents must take calls as they come in, the coaching plan called for the coaches to listen in on calls on a random basis and provide feedback at the termination of the call. This reinforced those things the agent was doing well, and provided suggestions on how to better deal with certain aspects of the call. In addition, when the agent got a call of the type that he or she usually did poorly on, that person could signal the coach to listen in and thus receive special help in learning to overcome the difficulty experienced. The program was quite successful in improving sales. To maintain the improvement, the regular supervisors were then trained to take over the coaching function as part of their regular duties.

Of course, managers are more than coaches. They must also be able to influence individuals whom they are not coaching. They must be able to influence their peers, and they must also be able to influence their superiors. But because our focus in this volume is team building, we will limit our discussion to influence as it relates to team members. Besides, the skills of the effective team leader, since they are skills in influencing human behavior, apply to influencing peers and superiors as well as team members.

Influencing the Group

Studies by Rensis Likert and others have shown that when a manager tries to deal with people exclusively on a one-to-one basis, the subordinates do not develop into an effective team. To become an effective manager one must be able to influence team members not only one at a time, but also all together at the same time. Looking ten people in the eye and trying to influence their behavior is obviously a quite different ball game from looking one person in the eye and influencing that person. For one thing, it takes much more energy to attend to the verbal and nonverbal responses of ten people than it takes to attend to only one. Second, the leader is faced with the very real possibility that everything he or she says is being interpreted somewhat differently by each of the team members because they all may be mostly concerned with the effect on themselves of whatever the leader may be saying. In addition, the team members often feel a sense of power when they are in a group meeting that they do not feel when dealing with the leader on a one-to-one basis. Group dynamics are at work. Since the usual purposes of whole-team meetings are to make sure that all members are equally well informed about task problems or progress, or to deal with group process problems, it is the leader's job to make sure that every member gets the message. Since, in any group, some members will grasp things much more slowly than others, it is extremely important that the leader does not make the mistake of communicating only to the swift. To influence the group the leader must communicate in a way that even the least experienced member of the team can understand clearly. The cardinal rule for leader communication was stated by General Curtis E. Lemay of the Strategic Air Command during World War II. It was called the *KISS* rule. KISS stands for "Keep it simple, stupid." Fortunately, most of the really important things a team leader is concerned with can be stated rather simply. Much of the effort directed at influencing the team as a whole is aimed at improving the group process, the way team members work together to achieve team objectives. As a consequence, the team manager is concerned with the enthusiasm the members have for the task at hand, with their commitment to the team goals, with the confidence they have in their own and their fellow team members' abilities, with their confidence in the leader, and with things of a similar nature. Since the question of influencing the group as a whole is really the question of leadership, the key to influencing a group lies in performing the functions of leadership previously discussed in this chapter.

The Principle of Interaction Influence

The principle of interaction influence was first discussed by Likert in his book, *New Patterns of Management.* It concerns the influence a manager can exert on the total organization of which his or her team is but one part, and the influence he or she can exert on subordinates. In a nutshell, the amount of influence a leader can actually have over team members is determined by how much the group is allowed to influence the leader. In other words, when a leader is willing to consider the opinions and the needs of team members to arrive at a decision or plan a course of action affecting the whole group, they will respond with strong commitment and involvement in carrying out the decision or the plan effectively. When the influence is allowed to flow *both* ways in the interaction between leader and team members, everybody feels like they own a piece of the action. *The interesting thing is that the team members are not gaining influence at the expense of the leader.* Everyone involved gains in influence, including the leader. There is simply much more influence being exerted in the organization. There is also much more energy generated within the team. This is because commitment and involvement means that the members believe their tasks and the group goal important enough to warrant putting a great deal of effort into meeting team objectives. Since this is what every leader tries to influence a team to do, it is evident that by allowing herself or himself to be influenced by the team, the leader has increased influence over them. On the other hand, consider the autocratic leader who ignores the opinions and needs of team members and rules with an iron hand. The best such a person can hope for from subordinates is obedience, often out of fear. The autocratic leader can never hope for commitment and involvement from team members. *People simply do not commit themselves to or get involved in activities they cannot influence.*

There is another aspect of the interaction principle that is equally important. To have maximum influence on the team, it is not enough that the leader allow himself or herself to be influenced by team members. That will secure initial commitment and involvement, but it will not necessarily sustain it. Whether the team allows the manager to maintain a high degree of influence on the team depends also on the extent to which he or she is able to exert influence upward on the boss and laterally on peer managers. In other words, the more clout the manager has upstairs and across the organization, the more influence that person will have with his or her own people. It seems rather apparent that a manager's influence on the larger organization of which the team is but one part will be limited by the effectiveness of his or her own team. Team members rightfully feel that in return for commitment, involvement, and extra effort their leader should be able to influence the organization enough so that they get their share of recognition, their share of the rewards, and the help and cooperation they need from other elements of the organization in order to do a bang-up job. If the leader fails to use the superior work the team is performing to exert influence on the organization, the team will reduce the amount of influence on their behavior that they have allowed. Winning teams demand winning leaders. Management is truly an influence game!

DEVELOPMENT AND APPLICATION
OF KEY SKILLS

All the management skills discussed in the preceding sections can be learned by nearly anyone willing to put forth the necessary effort. This does not mean that everyone can achieve the same level of skill. Not every prize-fighter becomes a Muhammad Ali. Nor is management everyone's cup of tea—nor should it be. After all, if everyone were managers, who would do the other work? But assuming that you are seriously interested in developing managerial skills, what are the key points to keep in mind?

There are four simple principles that you should keep in mind if you really, really want to develop organizational team-building skills.

Skills Are Learned by Doing

Reading about, studying about, and discussing how something is done, or even watching a skilled performer, can only provide information or knowledge. These methods may give you a pretty good idea of the sorts of things to consider, the kinds of things to watch out for, the general sequence of activities you should follow, and some things to try your first time out, but they cannot give you skill. You can become a skillful manager only by managing. You can develop team-building skills only by building teams. Practice is what it takes.

Skill Development Depends on Feedback

Without some way of knowing what you are doing right and what you are doing wrong, or which way is more effective and which less, you cannot improve your performance. Hence practice without provision for feedback, knowledge of the results of your effort, will not lead to skill improvement. You may be practicing the wrong thing. Imagine trying to learn to play the piano if you could not hear the sound. Whenever possible, find someone with the necessary expertise who is willing to coach you. Effective coaching, by providing guidance and feedback on your performance, will help you save a great deal of time and frustration in developing your skills.

Seek Opportunities to Develop Skills

Countless opportunities for developing management team-building skills exist. Often they can be had merely for the asking or by simply demonstrating a willingness to accept responsibility for getting something done. Most organizations that depend on volunteers are crying for people who will take the initiative, who will accept responsibility, and who will provide some leadership. Furthermore, they do not insist on expertise, only on good intentions. However, keep in mind the many facets of management team-building skill and choose your opportunities carefully so you will eventually develop all the component skills that make an effective manager. Recognize that many of the interpersonal skills may be developed in everyday, normal social interaction with friends and family.

Seek Opportunities to Apply Skills

Skills grow rusty with disuse. This is especially true of skills that have not been completely mastered. It is also probably true that in the area of interpersonal and team-building skills, no one can honestly lay claim to having fully mastered them. Providing that you receive the feedback necessary every time you apply your skills you can improve them. As a consequence, the more opportunities you can find in which to apply them, the better you will get.

It is worth noting that by embarking on a course of team-building skill development, you are engaging in what can be a lifelong learning experience. It can be an exciting, rewarding, and never-ending journey.

SUMMARY

This chapter discusses the manager's role as a team leader. Leadership is a learnable management skill that may be defined as the ability to influence the thinking, the attitudes, and the behavior of subordinates without use of coercion. Leadership is simply one kind of role that managers often have to take. It can be broken down into a number of specific behaviors or activities that taken together make up the role of leader. It is not necessary for the manager to always perform all of these activities of the leadership role personally, the manager's responsibility is to make sure that each of the functions that make up the leadership role are performed well enough by various group members so that team objectives will be met. Ten basic functions of the leadership role are presented. These are (1) establish, communicate, and clarify the goals; (2) secure commitment to the goals; (3) define and negotiate roles; (4) secure commitment to the roles assigned; (5) plan the activity and make it clear; (6) set performance standards and make sure they are understood; (7) provide feedback to individuals and to the group; (8) provide coaching and supervision; (9) provide initiative, enthusiasm, a sense of purpose, and an example of appropriate behavior and attitudes; (10) control the group climate and the group process. Sharing these leadership functions with other team members is the typical mode of management in high-performing groups.

Skill in influencing the thinking, the attitudes, and the behavior of others is the key skill a manager must learn if he or she hopes to develop high-performing teams. Influencing people one at a time is a distinctly different skill than influencing a group of people all at the same time. The coaching relationship is one powerful means by which the manager can influence all subordinates one at a time. The coaching relationship requires openness, honesty, respect, and trust. It also requires conviction on the part of the coach that the person being coached wants to perform at a higher level and is capable of doing so with appropriate help. Both coach and trainee must share the conviction that the coach actually has the skill to help improve performance. Whenever possible, the manager will share the coaching function with other members of the team who may be qualified to perform this service.

Influencing the group as a group is usually much more difficult than influencing individuals one at a time. Influencing the group as a whole boils down to the role of leadership. The key to influencing a group lies in performing the functions of leadership. The principle of interaction influence states that the amount of influence a leader possesses over team members is initially determined by how much the leader allows himself or herself to be influenced by them. To sustain influence over the group, the leader must also be able to exert influence upward and laterally in the organization.

All management skills can be learned. If you really want to develop organizational team-building skills, there are four principles to keep in mind. One, skills are learned by doing. Two, skill development depends on feedback. Three, you must seek opportunities to develop your skills. Four, you must seek opportunities to apply the skills you have developed to keep them from getting rusty.

ASSIGNMENTS

1. Using the definitions provided in this chapter, prepare an interview form that provides a section for interviewing a manager you know, or any manager who is willing to be interviewed, regarding the four basic functions of management: planning, organizing, leading, and controlling. In the interview, try to find out what kind of planning the manager must do, how he or she goes about it, about how often it must be done, and about how much time the manager spends on it. Try to find out similar information for the other three functions. Be sure to add a fifth heading, "Other", for any activities that do not seem to fit under the four basic functions.

2. In class discussion, present your results and compare them with the reports of other class members. How can you explain the similarities and differences?

REFERENCES

CASSTEVENS, E. R., AND LOVIN, B. C. *Coaching, Learning, and Action.* New York: American Management Association, 1971.

CRIBBEN, J. J. *Effective Managerial Leadership.* New York: American Management Association, 1972.

LIKERT, R. *New Patterns of Management.* New York: McGraw-Hill, 1961.

MCCLELLAND, D. C. *Power: The Inner Experience.* New York: Irvington Publishers, 1975.

MCCLELLAND, D. C., AND BURNHAM, D. H. "Power is the Great Motivator." *Harvard Business Review* 54, 2 (1976).

PANEL DISCUSSION

Page: It's obvious from the discussion on Chapter one that the role of management in planning interests us very much. Can we move on to some of the other functions of a manager's role, such as organizing, leading, or controlling? Would you like to tackle that, Shirley?

Chilton: One of the things I've noticed is that many managers classically and improperly take over functions in the execution role which should be performed by their subordinates. This is true to the extent that "I want to do it myself" or "I'm going to show you how to do it." You do not provide the subordinate with the opportunity to satisfy his own personal psychological needs. However, I have observed too often the situation where the manager has said, "Now I want you to do this," but the subordinate hasn't the foggiest idea of what he is supposed to do. And the reporting system is not outlined properly by the manager so that therefore nothing gets done. All you find is that people sort of stir around and shuffle paper and never get organized. The functions of training and education by the managers aren't properly performed. That's where I find the biggest decline in management technique; in getting the job done right then.

Page: That would be a function of faulty involvement of the subordinate in the planning process, involving specifically the "goals"—meaning those things that are very specific and quantified within a time frame and must be met, the "action steps" which everybody, the manager and his people, understands well. If we have that kind of involvement, then the subordinate, as well as the leader, will know.

Chilton: If that is accomplished at that point, then obviously it should be executed properly.

Ends: One of the most common complaints that I have heard from employees is just what you are speaking about, Shirley. The reason seems to go something like this: The manager assumes the employee knows what he means, the employee is afraid to ask because he feels the manager will say, "If you don't know what your job is, we don't need you around here." So he never asks and as long as no one complains about what he is doing, then he must be doing it right. I've heard this kind of statement in the lack of clear role definition or clear definition of expectations of the job from senior engineers who have been functioning as project leaders in industry ten or fifteen years. They still have this problem. For some reason, the communication lines are not open between the subordinate and the supervisor.

Kruel: I think that is a substantial problem. The other one I see more today is the necessity for the manager—I think that Dave said, "to be an architect"; I see it slightly different—as an engineer. He has to spend more time "engineering the bridge" between the individual's interest and the needs of his particular organization, finding ways to convince that individual that he should be part of this somehow and that the things that he is asked to do are good for him as well as good for the organization.

Covington: A good part of the problem, I believe, that I've run into in my own organization is that frequently there will be a situation where the manager has deadlines that he has to meet. He makes the job assignments and expects them to come back performed, and for one reason or another, it doesn't come back the way he wants it. I have a top manager who is as intelligent as anybody in my organization and he's a tremendous person intellectually. From a management standpoint he has a problem. He knows he can do a better job and get the work done faster than any of his subordinates, but many times he makes the work assignment and then all of a sudden we have a crisis situation, and he ends up doing it himself. Because he can do it better, he doesn't have to do the research that a subordinate has to do, but he's not performing his job as a manager as well as he should be.

Kruel: I think a lot of that depends on the level of the work function.

Covington: This is high level.

Kruel: Have you found that as the level of the work function increases you have people with greater intellectual training or skills, and they in turn generally require more freedom of choice?

Covington: Yes, and I give them freedom of choice. This level manager has absolute freedom to operate his area almost as he wants to. But he does have to manage instead of performing the subordinate tasks.

Chilton: One of my questions is: In your experience with team building, what skills are the hardest to learn, and how did you learn them? I'm supposed to be developing team-building skills, and you have just identified the thing that I have found hardest to do personally: I am impatient, I want to get the job done, I don't want to wait. I have found that the hardest thing for me to do is to let someone do the job and give them the opportunity to come back and present it.

Covington: Even if they do it wrong. They have to make mistakes to learn.

Chilton: Right! The question is: How did you learn them? So I devised and use the technique of developing the "reporting system", which is "controlling". They have to bring back certain reports and controls, which allow me to keep track of what they are doing, and, if they are going the wrong way, steer them more the way I think they should go. In addition, I also try to use "perpetual performance evaluation," complimenting them, saying, "Gee, that's fantastic!" or "You did a wonderful job over here on this." Maybe I'm leading up to, "Well, did you consider it this way?" or something I want them to do over. But that's the way I had to overcome my impatience in working with a team . . . if I know where they are through reports, I can keep the team together.

Kruel: There is a good point there. There are many tools you can use many ways. One tool which is extremely valuable is the organizational system. Many systems are so complicated that it is impossible to understand them, and the work flowing through the system ends up with little closed circuits accomplishing nothing. Consequently the system is perceived as a weapon rather than a tool. People usually try to do their best but they don't know what the system means or what it is trying to accomplish.

Ends: Does that imply that too many supervisors or managers really aren't devoting their time to developing other people?

Kruel: I think that's true, because people trying to accomplish things within an environment they don't understand often make their own decisions on what they think the system wants, and result in becoming frustrated because they are not sure. The supervisor should play a clear role in helping with the identity of the individual.

Covington: I think right now both in the public and private sector, we're going through a transition where we are trying to recognize this, and trying to do something about it.

Farrell: Your top manager's task is to transmit the expertise and information he has to the people under him.

Covington: It's a hard thing to do because his time is fully utilized, yet he has to do it. He can do it by setting an example in the way that he does things. The people under him can see what he does and learn that way, but that isn't going to be enough. They have got to get additional exposure, either through special training or assignment to various types of responsibilities.

Kruel: I found the earlier part of my business life was getting experience, but the later part of my business life is spent in trying to communicate my experience to someone else. That's a very difficult thing because you find yourself trying to superimpose that experience on them, hoping they will swallow it and use it immediately. But it just doesn't work that way.

Farrell: Perhaps because it's your experience and not their experience.

Kruel: Yes, that's right. And they don't benefit from it because they haven't been through it.

Covington: And maybe sometimes we're wrong. I know sometimes I'm wrong.

three

Key Concepts in Organizational Team Building

OBJECTIVES

After reading Chapter Three you should be able to:

1. Name some of the reasons why people resist change.
2. Discuss the power of expectations to influence behavior.
3. Outline the process by which adults change their behavior.
4. Describe the pattern followed by high achievers.
5. Identify the concept of organizational climate and what influences it.

INTRODUCTION

The previous chapter presented the manager's job as the application of a set of basic skills. In addition to a clear understanding of those skills, the would-be manager must be thoroughly familiar with five basic concepts that are vital in building effective organizations: (1) resistance to change; (2) the power of expectations; (3) the adult change process; (4) the achievement pattern and (5) the organizational climate.

RESISTANCE TO CHANGE

In the process of building an organization or increasing its effectiveness, the manager is constantly faced with the task of getting people to change their habitual ways of doing their jobs and thinking about their jobs. This is probably the most difficult part of any manager's job, because most adults resist change for a variety of reasons. Five of the most important reasons are (1) inertia, (2) the influence of past experience, (3) the influence of the person's self-concept, (4) the risk of failure, and (5) the perception of psychological disadvantage.

Inertia

The average adult is a creature of habit who is relatively comfortable with the way he or she does a job, with the way he or she looks at things, and the way he or she feels about things. These habits simplify life and enable us to conserve our physical, intellectual, and emotional energy for more interesting activities. Because changes in these habits generally require new learning, and learning may require considerable effort, reluctance to expend the necessary energy can by itself result in considerable resistance to change. It takes a fairly powerful stimulus to motivate an individual to overcome inertia. Clearly, unless one believes there is really some personal gain in it, one will not exert the effort.

The Influence of Past Experience

In addition to inertia, the past experience of the individual can exert a powerful force to resist change. This source of resistance arises from the fact that over the years a person's experiences have tended to support the belief that he or she is doing things the right way. We attribute the successes we have had in our work to the correctness of our methods and to their usefulness under all conditions. Every minor success supports this notion in our minds, and whatever failures we may have had we probably blamed on something else. When our methods are challenged, we can always recite a list of minor successes we have experienced while using those methods. We can also probably cite a number of reasons, other than our methods, for any failures. As a consequence, as long as our habits work reasonably well, and do not get us into serious trouble, we not only see no reason to change them, but also will strongly defend them.

The Influence of the Self-concept

A person's self-concept is simply an image of self. Not merely the physical image reflected in a mirror, but rather a set of psychological images that taken all together define in a person's own mind the kind of person he or she is or is trying to be. The process by which everyone steadily and consistently tries to establish, support, and add to this image of self is sometimes called *self-actualization.* For example, one may see oneself as a person of action, as a courageous leader, as an electronic genius, as a master craftsperson, or as any number of other images. These various self-images a person has are extremely important. Usually a person will willingly do those things that fit these images, that support them, or better yet, that add to or polish them a bit. The activities help actualize the self-concept. However, an image can also become a very potent source of resistance when one is asked to do something contrary to it. Normally people are very unwilling to act in a way that does not fit with their self-concepts. For example, a master mechanic or a perfectionistic typist may flatly refuse to do anything but a first-class job. From a managerial point of view, to avoid this source of resistance, one must know something of the way subordinates see themselves, and make sure that they see their assignments as compatible with their self-concepts.

The Risk of Failure

Fear of failure is a common, but seldom admitted source of resistance to change in adults. The way a person goes about doing a job usually is the result of much trial-and-error learning during which many mistakes were made. These mistakes may have been called to one's attention in a rather painful way by inconsiderate bosses or co-workers. Such experiences threaten one's self-concept by making one feel inadequate or stupid, a depressing and miserable experience at best. People pay a price in discomfort to learn how to do their jobs in the way that they do; therefore, when asked to learn a new way of doing something, especially if the change seems great, they may be very much concerned by the risk of failure. If they fail to learn as quickly as expected, or if they fail to learn the new way as well as expected, they know they will suffer. Not only may the self-concept be damaged, at least temporarily, but even worse, a person may lose the esteem of the boss and co-workers. The amount of risk a person is willing to take depends largely on that person's self-confidence and the consequences of failure as he or she sees them. Some people by nature seem to be willing to take very high risks, while others are unwilling to take any risks at all. People who have been badly burned by trying new ways of doing things usually will avoid risk, if at all possible, as a way of avoiding a repetition of a painful experience. Fear of failure as a source of resistance to change can be minimized by making sure that the changes are taken in small steps so that the risk is small. Perceived risk may also be kept to an acceptable level by assuring the person of coaching to help make the change.

The Perception of Psychological
Advantage or Disadvantage

The concept of psychological advantage refers to a person's private ideas about what is in his or her own best interests in any particular situation. While it may not always appear that way, people are constantly trying to serve their own best interests *as they see them*. What the individual thinks is best seems to depend on two things: (1) how the individual sees the job situation in terms of the rewards and punishments possible, and (2) how much the individual thinks he or she can influence the outcome by personal effort. For example, when asked to change the way you are doing your job, you size up the request taking both items (1) and (2) into account in your own way. If you then feel that you have more to gain than to lose by making the change, you will be motivated to do so. On the other hand, if you feel that you have more to lose than to gain, you will resist the suggested change because it is to your disadvantage. In weighing the possible gains and possible losses, we all give the greatest weight to those things that are most important to us at the time. For example, if we are very eager to acquire new skills, and think the change will offer that opportunity, we will make the change willingly. On the other hand, if we are very much afraid of failure, we resist changes that seem to offer much chance of failure, regardless of possible benefits.

For most ordinary everyday situations, people size up things and behave in terms of where they think their best interests lie, without being aware that they are doing so. Because of that, one should never *assume* that resistance to change is the result of careful, deliberate thinking and decision making. Often all the person is really aware of is a vague feeling that a suggested change is to his or her disadvantage. This source of resistance can often be avoided if the manager will only take the time to discuss suggested changes thoroughly with subordinates. The most critical objective of the discussion is to make sure that all subordinates clearly see that it is in their own best interests, and that of the organization, that it is to their psychological advantage, to make the suggested changes in behavior.

The first four sources of resistance to change can be regarded as frequent reasons why people decide a suggested change is not in their best interests. As a general rule, people will change their behavior when they are convinced it is to their advantage to do so, providing the gains *as they see them* clearly outweigh the risks as they see them, and as long as the rewards appear to be proportional to the effort required. Because no two people see it exactly the same way, the would-be manager must develop skill in understanding how the other person sees the situation. The skill of being able to put yourself in the other person's shoes is called *empathy*. Like all other management skills, it can be learned.

THE POWER OF EXPECTATIONS

Expectations may be thought of as assumptions, as predictions, as beliefs, or as prophecies we make about the outcome of events, our own behavior, or the behavior of others. Expectations are derived from our past experiences with similar situations or similar people. The more frequently the outcome of situations or the behavior of people matches what we expected, the more likely we are to enter new situations or new relationships with similar expectations. Expectations are among the most powerful factors that influence our behavior. We are influenced not only by our own expectations, but also by what other people expect of us. As previously mentioned, resistance to change or support for change depends largely on whether the person *expects* the outcome will be to his or her disadvantage or advantage. On the other hand, our responses to other people's expectations of us appears to be a more complicated affair. One of the reasons for this is that what people expect of us tells us something about how they regard us. As a manager, your expectations about the performance of your subordinates will have a profound effect on their behavior. Knowledge and skill in formulating, communicating, negotiating, and managing expectations can make the difference between success or failure as a manager. Let's examine some of the basic ideas about expectations.

The Self-fulfilling Prophecy

A person who expects to succeed in an endeavor probably will; a person who expects to fail almost certainly will. That statement represents the idea of the self-fulfilling prophecy in its simplest form. The reason it is that way is not hard to find. When a person expects to fail, that person usually doesn't try very hard to succeed. As a result, the likelihood of failure is high. We act as though our expectations are correct, and in so doing often create the result we expected. However, in an organization, the subordinates often are more influenced by the manager's expectations of their performance than by their own. The manager's expectations, which are communicated in many, often subtle ways can thus create a high-performance climate where everyone tries to do their best. On the other hand, if the manager expects employees to perform poorly, he or she creates a low-performance climate where few put forth more than minimal effort. In either case, the manager's expectations regarding the performance of subordinates, *if they are communicated in some way*, will usually be supported. Expectations thus tend to be self-fulfilling; they result in behavior that "proves" they were correct in the first place.

Communicating Expectations

Your expectations must be communicated if they are to have any influence on the behavior of others. Simply telling a subordinate what you expect is a good way to start. Management consultant Roger Harrison believes that no expectation is adequately communicated until it has been *written down* and is clearly understood by both sender and receiver, but expectations are communicated in many ways other than through the spoken and the written word (see Rockey, *Communicating in Organizations*, Winthrop Management Series). For example, if a manager tells a new employee that everyone is expected to be on time for work every day and to put in a full eight hours of work, the employee will probably believe that that is exactly what the manager expects. However, if the new employee soon discovers that most of the workers straggle in a half hour or more late and start leaving a half hour or more early with no reprimand or concern shown by the boss, the employee's ideas about the manager's real expectations soon change. In most cases, the new employee's behavior will soon change to conform to that of the rest of the employees. The boss has communicated what is *really expected* of employees by not reacting to their tardy behavior. If the manager refuses to accept anything but high-quality work from them, however, they soon realize that that is exactly what is expected of them. On the other hand, if the manager continually complains that employees spend too much time trying to get everything perfect, they soon know that the manager expects them to be more concerned with speed than with quality in doing their jobs. In the long run, it is the manager's consistant behavior toward the performance of employees that communicates these expectations to them.

Managing Expectations

The manager must develop skill in managing the expectations of subordinates. Otherwise, he or she may be accused of dishonesty, unfairness, or manipulation. This seems to be especially true with respect to rewards for special effort or for a tough job exceptionally well done. For example, an employee who voluntarily offers to take on extra work in addition to the regular assignment to help get a job done, often expects some kind of tangible reward for the extra effort. If the effort is substantial, the employee may envision a raise in pay or even a promotion, or at least some form of special consideration. Then, if the expected reward is not forthcoming, the subordinate feels he or she has been treated unfairly, even though no reward was ever promised. A person may feel that way because he or she was allowed to develop expectations of a reward when none was ever intended. The best way to avoid such problems is simply to discuss openly with the subordinate—before undertaking the extra effort—just what everyone expects to get out of it. That way, you have an opportunity to correct any unwarranted expectations.

Negotiating Expectations

A legal contract for work or services between two people may be thought of as a document defining exactly what each expects of the other. Contracts usually involve a great deal of negotiating before they are signed and become legally binding on both parties. Because such a legally binding contract seldom exists between manager and subordinates, the importance of negotiating expectations is perhaps even greater. The process of negotiation serves to get expectations out in the open where they can be examined by both parties and accepted, rejected, or modified as required. When both parties agree on what each can expect from the other, and make a commitment to live up to these expectations, a psychological contract has been "signed". The expectations that are subject for negotiation should include not only quality and quantity of work, but also should include such things as the amount of help, supervision, and coaching the manager will provide; the kind and amount of feedback the management will give the employee; the rewards and punishments used; the rate of progress expected in performance improvement; the amount of initiative the employee is expected to show; and the amount of responsibility the employee is expected to assume. Strange as it may seem, many not-too-successful managers assume that their employees know what is expected of them when, in fact, the employees are often afraid to ask. As a consequence, the subordinate may learn of the boss's expectations only after having fallen far short of them. That situation results in the manager being dissatisfied with the employee's performance and the employee being angry with the manager for not outlining what was expected. Or the employee may find that the boss expected much more than he or she felt able to deliver. Or the employee may have expected much more help from the boss than the boss expected to have to give. Such situations, which create distrust, hostility, disappointment, and low morale, can most easily be avoided by open negotiation of the expectations of both parties to the psychological contract. Uncommunicated, and therefore not negotiated, expectations are one of the major sources of conflict in interpersonal relations.

Expectations and Need Satisfaction

Our expectations regarding the behavior of another person have the greatest influence when the expectations as such satisfy some of the basic needs of the individual. For example, Gellerman has said, "If you want the best out of a man, expect it of him!" The reason that most people will try hard to live up to performance expectations is that the expectations satisfy some basic needs of the individual: the need of self-esteem and the need for the esteem of others. For instance, if you expect a subordinate to succeed in a very difficult task, one the person may feel is beyond his or her capabilities, you have helped satisfy that person's need for the esteem of others (yours in this case). Your subordinate will feel very good because you think so highly of his or her abilities. You have also offered the person a way to increase his or her self-esteem by performing at a higher level than ever before. At the same time your subordinate realizes that unless performance meets expectations, he or she will lose not only your esteem but also the opportunity to increase self-esteem. As a consequence, the employee will try hard to meet your expectations. There are several important points to keep in mind if your expectations are to have this constructive influence on the performance of subordinates. First your expectations must be just high enough above the subordinate's current level of performance so that he or she *can* meet them by stretching. Second you must be willing to provide the feedback and coaching required to help the person meet your expectations. Finally, as Gellerman has pointed out, successful managers are those who have discovered that faith in an individual often has to precede the justification for it.

THE ADULT CHANGE PROCESS

Developing skills, improving performance, increasing knowledge and awareness are all examples of the adult change process. The change process we are concerned with in this section is a learning process. *Learning* is a modification of behavior as a result of experience. While learning may result in either positive or negative changes in performance, depending on the person and the circumstances, managers are most interested in encouraging improvements in performance. To ensure that the learning situation will result in improved performance, the manager must have a good understanding of how adults learn and under what circumstances they are willing to set about trying to change their own behavior or job performance. Two general conditions must be met before an adult will accept a learning goal. The first condition is that the goal must not be threatening; in other words, the risk of failure must be low. The second condition is that the goal must be consistent with the person's self-image. If both of these conditions are met, the adult may be willing to embark on the four phases of the learning, or change, process itself.

The Conditions

The Nonthreatening Approach

Adults learn in small steps, and if strong defenses against changes have been built up, the first steps must be easily attainable, nonthreatening, and attractive. When each step is presented to the subordinate as a small, realistically attainable goal, it does not seem so formidable. Adults tend to be very cautious about learning experiences because failure would damage their self-images. This concern causes them to take only nonthreatening first steps, nonthreatening second steps, and so on. Especially in the early stages of deliberate learning attempts, adults learn in small, safe, easy steps. But what is easy varies a great deal from person to person. Remember, it is the subordinate's idea of what is small, safe, or easy that is important, not how the manager views it.

Self-actualization

Self-actualization is a term that refers to the process whereby people steadily and consistently try to establish, support, and add to their image of self. They will willingly do those things that fit this image, and will unwillingly do those things that do not fit. Therefore, to meet this condition for learning, the manager must present new learning so that it will help to establish, or actualize, the learner. This means that the desired learning process should help the learner to use his or her potential, to put it into productive action. The subordinate must see that new learning would help him or her to fulfill personal potential and live up to desires. The person must see the personal benefit in learning, that it will add to and support the image of self.

The Four-phase Process of Adult Learning

As pointed out by Lovin and Casstevens, the learning process consists of the four separate and usually consecutive steps outlined in the following sections.

Recognition of a Need

The adult will not put effort into trying to learn to improve performance unless he or she recognizes that old skills or knowledge or habits are somehow inadequate to achieve a higher level of performance. In other words, the employee recognizes a lack of something needed to perform better and thereby support a positive self-image. While this feeling of being somehow inadequate for the task at hand may make a person feel uncomfortable, useful learning cannot take place unless he or she proceeds to the next phase.

Precise Knowledge of What Is Needed

The person must somehow discover exactly what it is that is lacking. For example, if a sales manager tells a sales representative with a poor performance record to become a better sales person, the manager has not provided useful information. However, if he or she tells the salesrep that learning better closing techniques would improve his or her performance, then the salesrep would know exactly what skill to develop. Even this knowledge does not necessarily lead to improved performance, unless the subordinate moves into the next phase of the process.

Desire to Acquire What Is Needed

Once the adult knows exactly what he or she needs to learn in order to improve performance or take on a new task, the adult must really, really want to acquire that knowledge or skill or habit. The reason is simple: Unless the desire to learn is genuine, one will not put forth the effort it takes to acquire it. Having made the decision and the commitment to acquire what is needed, the adult must then move into the final phase of the learning process.

Need to Persist Until Skill Is Acquired

Until the subordinate actually begins expending energy to acquire the new knowledge or develop the skill no improvement in performance can be expected. Because skills are learned only by doing, and because skills are knowledge applied, the individual must usually start first by acquiring knowledge of "how to", then develop the skill required to apply that knowledge. For example, the salesperson mentioned would probably begin to develop improved closing techniques by reading one or two of the many books on·the subject, then go out and try to apply them. Gradually, with some coaching by the manager, this person would develop the skill to apply the knowledge gained from reading. To become good at it, he or she would have to keep putting forth the extra effort required until acquiring sufficient skill in closing to move performance more in line with the boss's expectations.

THE ACHIEVEMENT PATTERN

David McClelland and his co-workers have investigated the achievement motive extensively. While McClelland became primarily interested in changing the strength of the achievement drive, his approach was based on research studies that showed how people with strong drives for achievement behave. Though by no means the whole story of the achievement motivated individual, subsequent research on people with a high need for achievement showed certain consistent patterns of behavior. The three basic elements of the pattern which we refer to as the *achievement pattern* add up to a very practical formula for achievement or for improving performance in virtually any human endeavor. The three elements of the pattern are: (1) selection of goals, (2) selection of the achievement situation, and (3) insistence on feedback. While most high achievers seem to have learned the achievement pattern in the process of growing up, the principles can be learned and applied by anyone at anytime. An understanding of the achievement pattern and why it works can be very useful to any manager or team leader. Let's examine briefly each of three elements of the pattern.

Selection of Goals

The achievement-oriented person consistently selects goals that represent a moderate degree of risk. Such people choose goals that are realistic but still enough of a challenge to stimulate their best efforts. They avoid goals or improvement targets that are either too easy or too risky. While some people prefer the wild speculative gamble, others prefer a conservative approach that minimizes the risk of loss or the threat of failure. The high achievers are somewhere in between. Compared to the average person, the high achiever is not nearly as conservative. He or she is a firm believer in the maxim, "Nothing ventured, nothing gained." While the goals set may appear to be quite risky to an onlooker, the achievement-oriented person sets goals very carefully with respect to his or her self-confidence in the ability to achieve them by exerting a reasonable amount of effort and skill. The goals therefore represent a level of performance for which the high achiever is willing to hold himself on herself accountable. This type of goal-setting behavior is closely related to the next element in the achievement pattern.

Selection of Achievement Situations

French, McClelland, and others found that high achievers preferred situations in which they were personally responsible for the outcome of the projects they undertook, rather than situations in which the outcome was largely dependent on luck. They sought out situations where their personal efforts, skills, abilities, and determination stood a reasonable chance of influencing the outcome. It should be noted that "skills and abilities" are not confined to technical or business know-how, but also include such things as the ability to promote a product or an idea, and skill in influencing the behavior of others.

By picking situations in which individual effort will largely determine success or failure, the high achiever literally puts his or her self-image on the line. It is rather easy to see now why the high achiever prefers moderate risks. Awareness of the risk and knowledge of one's ability to influence the outcome work together to produce and ensure commitment to the goal. To even further ensure successful completion of the undertaking, the high achiever insists on one other form of insurance, the final element in the pattern.

Insistence on Feedback

High achievers select situations which not only meet the requirements of element (2) above, but that have the added characteristics of providing immediate and concrete feedback. In other words, once a high achiever embarks on a project, he or she wants to know how well performance meets expectations. This person needs some way of measuring progress toward goals. He or she must also know what is going right and what is going wrong so that performance can be adjusted accordingly. The kind of feedback that is provided is quite important to the achievement-oriented person, who wants feedback on performance to be as objective, as concrete, and as immediate as possible. This insistence on *objectivity* means that the person wants to know *exactly* what he or she is doing wrong or not doing well, as well as what he or she is doing right or very well. This desire for *concrete* feedback means that the person prefers not to depend on the opinions and evaluations of others to tell how he is doing. The high achiever would rather be able to count widgets coming off the assembly line, or add up total sales for the day, or calculate cost figures precisely so as to personally determine progress toward the goal. This strategy greatly reduces the risk of human bias or human error in the feedback such a person depends on to correct or improve performance. The concern for *immediate* feedback, of course, allows one to modify performance very rapidly if one is doing the wrong thing or is not on target. No achievement-oriented individual likes to waste energy and other resources doing the wrong thing. As many research studies in learning have demonstrated, the sooner knowledge of results of a performance is provided to a learner, the faster that individual can learn. High achievers have learned how to learn from their own experience. In a very real sense, they have discovered how to coach themselves.

THE ACHIEVEMENT PATTERN AND
THE ADULT CHANGE PROCESS

Both the adult change process and the achievement pattern deal with ways in which people learn to improve their performance on the job. By combining the two concepts, we can develop a very useful checklist for a team leader to follow in coaching subordinates to higher performance. If applied carefully over a reasonable period of time, it may also help the subordinates develop the behavior patterns of the achiever. The checklist is most useful in the joint goal setting and planning that is part of any serious coaching attempt.

The Coaching Checklist

1. Does the subordinate really believe he or she needs the knowledge, skill, or ability being considered?
2. Does the subordinate understand precisely what is needed?
3. Does the subordinate really want to acquire the skill?
4. Will the subordinate have personal responsibility for the outcome of the event or will the outcome be determined largely by forces over which he or she has little or no control?
5. Are the goals realistic but challenging for the subordinate considering his or her ability, experience, and self-confidence? Or are they too easy, or too risky?
6. Will the situation provide sufficient immediate, objective, concrete feedback so the subordinate can determine how well he or she is doing?

TEAM DEVELOPMENT

Development or improvement of individual team members' performances is the foundation on which all successful team development is based. The chief difference between individual and team performance is that in team performance a very critical ingredient has been introduced. This is the ability of the team members to work together as parts of a single organism. This additional requirement makes the job of the coach as well as the job of each team member more difficult in some ways but easier in others, as we shall see in Chapter 4. However, the coach may use the same coaching checklist for teams that is used for individuals by simply substituting the word "team" for the word "subordinate" in the list. The coach must recognize, however, that what is needed will often be things like "greater skill in working together."

THE ORGANIZATIONAL CLIMATE

The concept of *organizational climate* refers to a set of values, attitudes, and traditions that affect the way people relate to each other in accomplishing the work of the organization. The climate of an organization is sometimes called the *internal social environment*, or the *motivating environment*. It has been given many labels. It is an important concept because it helps explain, for example, why in some organizations the workers are against management, while in other organizations they are with management all the way. The "climate" as felt or perceived by the individual worker has a strong influence on on-the-job behavior. It affects the amount of work workers are willing to do. It affects the amount of initiative and ingenuity they are willing to display. It affects their willingness to commit themselves to high-performance goals. It affects their attitudes toward taking risks. It also affects their attitudes toward supervisors, peers, subordinates, and even toward themselves.

As you might expect, in large organizations the climate may vary considerably from one department to another. Employees in a large retail store, for example, may think the camera department a great place to work, while they may see the jewelry department as a perfectly miserable place to work. Thus, even though the overall characteristics of the climate in an organization are determined by the top management, one of the most significant persons setting the climate the worker responds to is his or her immediate supervisor, the work-team leader. Except in extremely autocratic and rigid organizations, the supervisor and managers usually are given a great deal of leeway in managing their people. By their own actions toward subordinates they can influence the climate as experienced by subordinates and thereby greatly influence group performance. A better understanding of the concept of climate, its importance, and its major determinants can be gained by a brief consideration of the concept as it appears to a single work team. We will consider five major determinants of the organizational climate in a group or team: (1) the value system, (2) patterns of power and authority, (3) group morale and cohesiveness, (4) openness in communications, and (5) intergroup relations.

The Value System

The term *value system* refers to those things that the group members believe are very important to them. Performance goals that are mutually agreed on by team members as important enough to work hard to attain are one type of value. Accepted behavioral norms which indicate how members are to interact with one another and with outsiders are another type of value. Dress codes may reflect a third type of group value. Certain attitudes toward the team leader may also represent part of the group value system. Even political or religious preferences may become woven into the group value system.

Because the value system reflects what most group members think is important to them, it tends to become a yardstick. It is a set of expectations about the behavior, attitudes, feelings, and performance of each team member that defines what is acceptable and what is unacceptable. Acceptance of the value system becomes a condition of group membership. Violation of the value system typically results in some form of punishment. In some cases the member may be thrown out of the group. In general, groups will reward members whose behavior is consistent with the group value system and punish those whose behavior is not.

For the aspiring team builder, it is quite important that all team members subscribe to the same work-group value system. If they do not, at worst the members may never jell as a team. At best, the team leader may have a great deal of additional work to do in resolving conflicts between members. By way of illustration, consider a six-person work team assembling digital voltimeters. Each worker has a distinctly different assembly task, but all six are needed to complete the assembly of the voltimeter. If three of the team feel that speed of production is the most important value, while the remaining three feel that quality of production is the more important value, a major conflict in value systems exists. Such conflicts can divide the six-person group into two opposing groups that can disrupt production entirely. The speedy group will complain that they are made to look bad because they have to wait for the others in order to do their job, resulting in low output. The quality group may complain that the speedy group is careless and makes them look bad because so many voltimeters are rejected by final inspection. Team-building efforts have failed because of lesser conflicts in value systems.

Many of the values that are important in a team or work-group activity tend to be those of the individuals involved and cannot be easily influenced by either the leader or the other group members. The message for the team builder is clear: If you have a choice, pick team members who already hold the key values necessary for successful performance on your team. For example, if successful team performance will require a great deal of initiative by each member in making cold calls, try to select members who place a high value on that kind of initiative. Or if successful performance requires painstaking attention to detail, try to select team members who already place a high value on very careful work. The more the members' "built-in" values match the requirement of the team task and are similar among group members, the less persuading the leader must do and the fewer internal conflicts will crop up.

Patterns of Power and Authority

A second major element that helps establish the climate in an organization is how power and authority are exercised and who actually possesses them. Simply put, *authority* is the right to give orders or directions, make decisions, assign tasks, and the like. It goes with the job, and the limits are usually spelled out in the job description of every supervisor or manager. *Power*, on the other hand, may be thought of as the ability to influence the behavior of others in some desired way. Authority is a characteristic of the position, while power tends to be a characteristic of the individual. A manager may or may not have the power to exercise legitimate authority. The dilemma faced by every manager or team leader is how to acquire the power to match authority. The methods he or she uses in trying to resolve the dilemma have a significant impact on the organizational climate from the subordinates' viewpoints. Fortunately, extensive research by Rensis Likert and his associates have provided some useful guidelines for dealing with this age-old problem.

Group Morale and Cohesiveness

The third major element that helps determine the organizational climate consists of the attitudes of the team members. Two types of attitudes are important. One set of attitudes is concerned with how team members feel about the ability of the team to achieve its goals, to successfully complete challenging or difficult tasks, or to win in a competitive situation. The feeling of team members that they belong to a winning team is referred to as "high morale"; if team members feel they are on a losing team, they have low morale. Because these feelings or attitudes are closely related to the expectations the team members have about their ability to perform as a team, they operate in much the same way. They can become self-fulfilling prophecies. For this reason, every team leader, coach, or manager keeps a watchful eye on the morale of the team. A team that expects to lose has lost the game before it starts.

The second set of attitudes is concerned with how each team member feels about the rest of the team members. If all team members like to be with and work with the rest of the team members, the result is a highly cohesive group. They will tend to stick together simply because they like each other's company. The team members have developed emotional ties with one another. While it is obviously much more pleasant to work with people you like and who feel friendly toward you and toward each other, cohesiveness is important for another reason. For example, if some team members do not like each other it tends to divide the team into two or more opposing groups. This result usually seriously downgrades group performance. However, a group may be highly cohesive and still not get anything done. Members may spend most of their work time socializing.

Both high morale and cohesiveness are characteristic of high-performance teams. The effective team builder and team leader must develop the skills required to develop both of these attributes in any collection of individuals he or she hopes to weld into a high-performing team. To keep the distinction between these two sets of attitudes in mind, one can think of cohesiveness as the attitudes and feelings that hold a group together voluntarily. It is related to the process function discussed in Chapter 1. Similarly, one can think of morale as the attitudes and feelings a group has about its own ability to get a job done. It is related to the task function discussed in Chapter 1.

Openness in Communication

The fourth major element affecting the organizational climate is the openness of the communication among members of the organization. Basically *openness* refers to the freedom team members feel about expressing their ideas, opinions, and feelings about both the task and process functions in the work situation. These include such things as feeling it is safe to ask questions about how to proceed, or why something is done in a specific way. They also include how free people feel to suggest new approaches or better ways of doing things. Perhaps most important of all is the extent to which subordinates feel free to discuss such things with superiors. Far too often openness is confined to communication among subordinate team members. The team leader or manager may never be told what he or she needs to know because subordinates are afraid to talk to the boss. Under such circumstances, the subordinates may form a tightly knit, cohesive group which excludes the leader from membership. In that case, the leader's effectiveness suffers, and inevitably team performance will suffer because of the breakdown in communication and the mistrust it generates. Openness in communication is vital to enable the team to draw on all the knowledge, talent, and ability that the various group members may possess. To the extent that openness among team members, including the leader, is reduced, not only will performance potential be reduced but morale and cohesiveness as well. These elements are all interrelated. For example, when morale is low, communication usually becomes quite guarded. When communication is guarded, cohesiveness deteriorates because team members lose trust in one another. They no longer know what the other person is thinking and feeling.

As might be expected, the degree of openness in team communication is greatly influenced by the leader. It is influenced primarily by the example the leader sets in communicating with subordinates. It is secondarily influenced by attitudes and feelings group members hold toward each other. Finally it is influenced by the climate in the larger organization of which the team is a part.

Intergroup Relations

The fifth major factor that creates the organizational climate is the character of the working relationships among the various teams that make up the larger organization. Do the various teams work together as members of an even larger team? Or do they all work independently with little regard for the needs and goals of any team but their own?

Most organizations can be thought of as an assembly of

highly interdependent teams, each with its own special function to perform. If the organization is to achieve its objectives efficiently, all of the many teams should work together smoothly. That requires a great deal of cooperation and coordination between and among the various parts of the enterprise. Just as conflict or hostility among individual team members will seriously impair team performance, conflict between teams will impair overall organizational performance. Intergroup conflicts are the bane of larger organizations and often result in costly power struggles between opposing teams. While the real or imagined threat from the other teams may result in high cohesiveness and solidarity within a team, it denies the team the possibility of high performance. The reason for this is that no team in an organization is truly independent. The performance of each is to some extent dependent on the other teams in the organization. In general, the same principles involved in developing single teams apply to organizations made up of many teams. Many of the same techniques are used, but with modifications to cope with the complications due to the greater number of people involved. As a result, basic team-building skills are the foundation on which higher-level management skills are built.

SUMMARY

In this chapter we discussed five basic concepts with which the aspiring manager should be thoroughly familiar. An understanding of these concepts is vital in building effective organizations. These concepts are: (1) resistance to change; (2) the power of expectations; (3) the adult change process; (4) the achievement pattern; and (5) the organizational climate.

Five major sources of resistance to change were discussed. The first of these was inertia. This simply means that it takes less energy to operate on the basis of habit than to learn new ways of doing things. Hence most people will not exert the necessary effort unless the rewards appear large. The influence of past experience was the second source of resistance to change. Whatever success the individual has had he or she attributes to the methods used, and is therefore reluctant to change them. Another source discussed was the person's self-concept. A person will not willingly act in a way that does not seem to be compatible with his or her self-concept. The risk of failure was identified as a common but seldom admitted source of resistance to change in adults. Adults tend to accept change only when it is presented as a series of small, safe steps. The final source of resistance to change discussed was the perception of possible psychological disadvantage associated with the change. This refers to the fact that people evaluate a proposed change in terms of whether it seems to be in their best interest. If not, resistance follows.

The power of expectations was explored. The concept of the self-fulfilling prophecy refers to the fact that expectations often influence a person's behavior and the behavior of others in a way that justifies the expectations. Expectations are communicated to others in many direct and subtle ways. But it is the manager's consistent behavior toward the performance of employees that most clearly communicates the manager's expectations to them. The team leader must manage the expectations of team members. This is especially true concerning anticipated rewards for extra effort. Unwarranted expectations should be prevented from developing. Since both the team leader and the team members have expectations regarding the job performance of the others, rewards should be openly and honestly negotiated. This will minimize disappointment on both sides. A manager's expectations have the greatest influence on the team when they satisfy basic individual needs such as the need for esteem.

The adult change process is a four-step process by which job-related learning takes place. First the individual must be aware of a lack of some skill or knowledge necessary to better performance. Next the person must be able to identify exactly what is needed to improve performance. However, these two steps will not effect a change unless the individual really, really wants to acquire the needed skill or knowledge. The final step is taking action to acquire it, and sticking with it until the desired goal is reached.

High achievers are people who have discovered a formula for achieving the goals they set for themselves. The achievement pattern contains three major elements. The first is setting challenging but achievable goals. The second is picking situations where the outcome is dependent on personal effort rather than chance. The third includes making sure that concrete and immediate feedback on performance is available. This pattern can be combined with the steps in the adult change process to provide a good coaching checklist for a manager or team leader.

The organizational climate refers to a set of values, attitudes, and traditions which strongly affect the way people work together in an organization. Five major determinants of climate were identified. The value system is one of the most important. It refers to those things that the group believes are very important to them, such as performance norms or social norms. Groups tend to enforce their value systems. Climate is also affected by the patterns of power and authority in the organization. Authority is the *right* to control the performance of others, while power is the *ability* to control the performance of others. An effective manager must have both. If not, tension and inefficiency permeate the organization. Group morale and group cohesiveness also affect the climate. Both are usually present in high-performing groups. Where both high morale and strong cohesiveness exist, another determinant of climate usually is in evidence. This is openness in communication among members of the group, including the team leader. The final determinant of climate we discussed was how the various groups in the organization get along with one another. Cooperation or conflict between groups greatly influences the organizational climate, and so the behavior of the people working in it.

ASSIGNMENTS

A. Empathy and Feedback Exercise

1. Pair off with a class member whom you do not know well.
2. Interview each other by asking the following three questions.
   a. What have you learned in this course so far?
   b. What do you want to learn by the time the course is finished?
   c. What are you going to do to make sure that you learn what you want by the end of the course?
3. Listen very carefully to your partner's answers. Try to put yourself in that person's shoes as you listen, and try to understand how he or she really feels about the answers. Do not write the answers down. Simply pay full attention.
4. Report to the class as though you were the person you interviewed. Start with, "I am (other person's name). What I have learned so far in this course is _____."
   Do the same for all the questions. Do not try to repeat the exact words you heard. Try to convey the other person's meaning and feelings as accurately as you can.
5. Ask the person you interviewed whether your report accurately reflected his or her meaning and feelings. If not, where did you miss?
6. Ask the rest of the class how well they thought you were able to empathize with the person you interviewed.

B. Expectation Exercise

1. Pair off with a class member or friend whom you know very well.
2. Without prior discussion, each person is to make out two lists of no more than ten items each. One list contains your most important expectations regarding your friend's behavior toward you. The other list contains what you think your friend expects of you.
3. Compare lists and discuss. Do your expectations agree? Do you need to negotiate your expectations of each other? Were you surprised?

C. Achievement Pattern Exercise

Following the principles discussed in the section on the Achievement Pattern, write a plan to achieve a goal that is personally important to you and that can be completed within one month. Be sure your plan provides all of the elements of the achievement pattern. Put your plan into practice and keep a log of your activity and results. Prepare a report on the exercise.

REFERENCES

CASSTEVENS, E. R., AND LOVIN, B. C. *Coaching, Learning, and Action.* New York: American Management Association, 1971.

GELLERMAN, SAUL W. *Motivation and Productivity.* New York: American Management Association, 1963.

HARRISON, ROGER. "Role Negotiation: A Tough-Minded Approach to Team Development." In Warren G. Bennis, et al. (Eds.), *Interpersonal Dynamics*, 3rd ed. Homewood, Ill.: The Dorsey Press, 1973.

KOLB, DAVID A. "Changing Achievement Motivation." In Warren G. Bennis, et al. (Eds.), *Interpersonal Dynamics*, 3rd ed. Homewood, Ill.: The Dorsey Press, 1973.

LIKERT, RENSIS. *The Human Organization: Its Management and Value.* New York: McGraw-Hill, 1967.

PANEL DISCUSSION

Ends: Why don't we start this discussion by asking Bob to make the opening statement?

Covington: Chapter Three points to and emphasizes the way in which we can improve the organization by improving the employees ability to function. I believe in addition to that, it has indicated a lot of the pitfalls as well as some of the methods that managers can use to accomplish this. But I believe that it is equally important and perhaps a key to success that the manager himself have the right attitude. The influence that he can exert can determine whether or not changes in the organization are going to be successful. The manager has to have a positive attitude. He's got to be reasonable in defining his goals and objectives. He's got to have enthusiasm, and he has got to be able to instill this in the employees that he is working with. He has to want change, not just for change's sake, but because through change he can accomplish goals and bring about the success of the program he is trying to install.

Ends: But Bob, how do you manage to instill your enthusiasm in the fifty or so different departments that make up the typical county government?

Covington: Well, it was really impossible. With fifty different managers an administrator has an impossible task of communication and span of control. But within the past few years I've been able to convince our Board of Supervisors that we needed to recognize that we had an impossible communication problem and an impossible management condition. So we've begun reorganizing into agencies. It reduces my span of control from about fifty departments to about eight agency heads. In this way we've been able to improve the operational structure of the county to get department heads working together. We've used the team concept that is perhaps one of the most discussed subjects in this chapter. To accomplish this, the agency heads are part of my team. They meet with me every week and we try to solve our problems. We try to establish our goals and do our planning. We still haven't completed this reorganization yet. You don't make this kind of rather revolutionary change in a political situation without a lot of traumatic experience. We have elected department heads as well as appointed department heads, so there are many of the problems that are mentioned in Chapter Three that we get involved in—both at the higher and the lower levels of government.

Ends: Bob, in the first part of your statement you indicated that a manager has to have a good positive attitude to be able to communicate enthusiasm and such. I certainly agree with that. But how much value do you really see in having a reasonably thorough understanding of what the behavioral science principles are all about? Do they help the manager understand how to deal with people and how to get them to produce?

Covington: I think that is an important aspect of it. I don't think that enthusiasm alone will accomplish it. Enthusiasm was just one of the things that wasn't emphasized, and I think it is very important. You have mentioned the positive aspects and the need to overcome the resistance which is sometimes prevalent when you try to make changes.

Page: Resistance to change is perhaps the most natural thing in the world. Once we get this human organism in balance, we resist changing whatever it is that keeps it in balance. That seems to be true whether its our eating habits, our schedule, or whatever; we simply want to keep it that way. Anything that is being handled reasonably well and is in balance has some kind of equilibrium which resists change.

Covington: Yes, if everybody is comfortable the way things are, then they don't want to change. But I'm not sure that in business, nor in government, that everybody is comfortable. In fact, in government I think by virtue of the nature of legislative bodies we're in a constant state of discomfort.

Kruel: I think that's very interesting. I think we tend to strive for achieving happiness for everyone. But the only ones that really want change and try to promote change are the ones that are unhappy. So, you know, I think it is just as important to have some unhappy people working for you as well as happy people.

Covington: I'm not sure that happy or unhappy are the right terms. I think of satisfaction and dissatisfaction. I think many people are striving for something more than they have, in job satisfaction, in their own improvement, in wanting to do something other than they are doing. With that kind of condition, then you have the elements of change. But if you have a condition where everybody is doing exactly what he wants to do, and everyone is completely satisfied, then they certainly are going to resist change.

Kruel: Well, I have to admit that in my youth when I had less, I was a greater radical. (laughter)

Covington: Well, personally I am a very conservative person and yet I enjoy change because I do see so many things that can be improved. I am always trying to change things in my organization. Sometimes to the frustration of those I work with.

Farrell: I certainly found out in my situation that one of the problems I'm having to deal with in our organization is this attitude toward change. The company has had an outstanding record of success. Profits have been quite good and growth has been running about 35 to 45 percent a year. I've got so many managers saying, "What in the hell are you messing with the system for? Leave us alone, we are doing just great." So you've got to look at turnover and absenteeism and some other less obvious indicators of a need for change. Satisfaction and resistance to change is different from level to level within the organization.

Kruel: I wonder if you have done any work testing for sensitivity to change in an organization? By that I mean that as time goes on a person's desire to change tends to diminish in relationship to how comfortable things are for him.

Covington: I wonder also if there is a difference, if there is a measurable difference or a correlation to the level of the particular person, whether he's top management or the lowest level?

Page: It appears that some human beings have more of a need for change than others, and although what I said about the basic organism and resistance to change in terms of messing with the equilibrium holds, we do note that if we are in equilibrium, in some kind of total balance, there is something about the human being which motivates us to deliberately set out to upset that balance. We deliberately seek change. It appears that it is a seeking of excitement or it may be a seeking of proving to ourselves that we can get it out of balance and put it back in.

Farrell: Life is change. The only way to stop changing is to die.

Covington: I think your description of change related to excitement is valid. This is true for the individual who becomes excited because something new happens.

Chilton: Some people relate to change as the only way they know they are growing. Growth represents change. One of the things I get involved with all the time is the cultural change in the position of females. They say, "We've got to change our whole way of life because we've had some people saying this is what we need." And yet there are vast numbers that don't want a thing to do with change. It is particularly true in business. I found that the females come to me and say, "Gee, I think I want to do something different," because they think this is the thing to do. They don't feel "with it" unless they say, "I want to get more involved in department management or management training." I respond with, "Well, all right, let's sit down and talk about that. What areas do you feel you would be interested in? What turns you on?"

Unfortunately, when I have found women who I thought were talented and very brilliant people, I've said, "I have an opportunity for you." But my experience has been that 98 percent of the time, given the opportunity, it's been declined with, "Oh, I don't want that responsibility; gee whiz, I didn't think you were really going to do that." They didn't want the change!

Ends: I think that many people are trying to live up to somebody else's role expectations, rather than trying to be themselves and to find their own roles and their own need satisfactions, their skills and ability, and what they really want out of life. This, I think, is one of the keys to team building, trying to find out what that person really wants, not what he thinks somebody else thinks he should be. I expect for so many years so many women have thought about their role as homemaker or whatever, and they feel somehow they're lacking because they are not really taking the role that so-called modern women are expected to fulfill. And yet when they're really faced with the choice they say, "That isn't really what I want."

Chilton: It's a problem that business and organizations have facing them, and its a real one. It's very sad to see so many women and young girls think they've got to change because it's the "in" thing. They're having great conflict and its creating conflicts in organizations because they don't know what to do with these people. Frankly, many of them don't know what to do with themselves.

Kruel: I think another aspect of that question comes to me a different way. You wonder how many times in any given organization we work with a person as a person versus that person as he or she wants to be.

Farrell: Or as you need him to be.

Kruel: If you deal with the wrong thing you can spend a long time going up a blind alley.

Covington: That was one of the things that was emphasized —that you have to lead people along gradually. If you try to move them too fast or take too big a step, they feel threatened or they feel that they might fail, and they don't want to fail because if they fail, why then they're in real trouble. So you do a little bit at a time.

Chilton: That's an extremely good point.

Ends: Do you think a manager really has any responsibility for helping people define their own roles in the work world?

Covington: Sure. If you have these people as employees and your organization is going to be successful in getting the performance from them, you've got to try and find out what they're best in and try to get them into that slot, and that isn't easy.

Ends: Particularly if they don't have a very good handle on it themselves.

Covington: Ten years ago, very little in government ever involved participation in terms of financing for employee training. But we are almost to the opposite extreme now. In our county we have what we call our training and learning center, which only serves San Bernardino County. This is one of the ways in which we help the employee to determine what he can do best and give him the broad exposure that he wouldn't otherwise have a chance to get. Right now, we probably will spend $50,000 this current fiscal year for this purpose. Considering that about six years ago we spent about $2,000, that's a pretty big change.

Ends: Isn't much of that money spent on formal education rather than really coming to grips with what I, as an employee, really want out of life and what I am capable of doing?

Covington: I think probably 75 to 80 percent of it is formal education, but we do have a number of courses which we conduct ourselves. Much of our training is right in our own buildings in our Training and Learning Center. We have a number of courses which are pointed toward the individual in trying to help him see what he wants to do.

Ends: Well, is that in lieu of the employee's supervisor actually helping him work through some of his problems? I know it's a very time consuming thing and many training programs set up in organizations are designed to unload the manager and make him feel that he has done his duty by the employee; and if the employee doesn't take it and translate it into on-the-job behavior, that's tough.

Covington: I think you're right. In many instances in our own organization, I'm sure that's true. However, we have organized it in a way so that every employee involved in training, in his semiannual work performance evaluation, has to set forth the goals that he has as he sees them himself, and the evaluator discusses this with him and they try to agree on these goals. Then each department has to submit to the training center, each year, a department plan for training. So it is a formalized procedure. I won't say that we are getting all the success that we should, but we're really just getting underway—we're learning ourselves.

Chilton: So you really think it's a good idea that we have a formal "Let's sit down and talk about where you're going" session? I personally don't utilize that technique because I like to do it as an ongoing thing, because the actual performance of sitting down and saying, "We're now going to sit down and discuss this," can be a threatening situation.

Covington: It can be.

Kruel: I look at that a little differently. I think that in order to have the person work successfully within the organization, it's important to know what this person expects from the organization, and whether the organization can satisfy that expectation. And if you don't deal with that, you are overlooking the reason a person likes or dislikes his work. You must find some means of exciting the person to believe that his expectations are achievable, or redirect his expectations. If they don't believe that what they want is achievable, then I think the person kind of works in a vacuum.

Chilton: I agree with you 100 percent. I don't like the formal every six months or once a year discussions only. I do this constantly.

Kruel: I think that as things come up, the approach should be to discuss them then.

Chilton: I do too—you can move somebody along faster. You may find you really have a gem and you need him, so let's cultivate that now.

Covington: Well, it depends on the size of the organization too. In a large organization, to be sure that it is done, you have to have a formal procedure. I agree with you 100 percent that when an employee does something worthwhile, he ought to know about it at the time that he does it, not six months later. And when the company, or the government, or whatever, is doing something momentous, they should let the employees know when they are doing it and not let them read about it in the newspaper when that is possible.

Ends: Walt, what percentage—just an off-the-top-of-your-head figure—of the managers that you know do you think really do a good job of developing their people, and about how much time do you think they devote to it?

Kruel: Well, being a purist, it's hard to give a percentage, but I would say a very high number of managers are oriented toward satisfying their own needs more than they are toward recognizing the needs of the people below them. They do communicate things the manager thinks should be, such as, "You're not meeting my objectives," and so on, but I perceive good development to mean staying in close understanding with and trying to negotiate differences between the individual and the organization. I think only a small number of managers spend enough time in real development of people.

I don't think they see development quite as important as they see the importance of job function. The belief that it is necessary to devote more time to development, I think, is held by a small number of managers—and by small I mean maybe 15 to 20 percent.

Page: One of the questions I had was whether or not you people have had learning as a conscious process for you, in terms of the adult change process. It interests me as to how conscious you may have been of the learning process and what you've gone through in terms of bringing change within yourself.

Covington: Well, I don't feel that I have ever been reluctant to try to do anything. I've never felt threatened or that I had to take only a little step at a time, but I think it depends a lot on the individual. I've always had enough self-confidence so that I would be glad to try anything, but if I didn't succeed, I'd try something else. I know that that isn't true with everybody, but I do have a number of people in my organization that are the same way.

Kruel: My feeling for learning has partly been subconscious and partly something I realize when I do something foreign, something different from the way I used to do it. This is really sort of a hard thing for me to bring out, but I think the most conscious realization I have of learning is when I'm exposed to things that I am not completely familiar with. When I do have the confidence I know them, I don't think I learn anything, but when I don't have the confidence that I think I know them, then I feel that I should stop and listen, and I spend more time listening until something sinks in.

Chilton: I know—it's wonderful! I must fit into that category. There isn't any time when I don't want to be exposed to something new that is available that I think I can learn from. I don't know of an occasion when I haven't benefitted from the exposure. Well, it's hard for me to explain too. It is just a desire to keep learning. I hope I'll feel this way when I am ninety years old. It's so vital to me.

Covington: Well, you have the enthusiasm I was talking about.

Kruel: I want to make a note or comment about the high-achiever aspect of things. It is always an intriguing thing to me because I often wondered why some people want to do things, as a way of feeling a sense of achievement, while others do not. I found at times that people reach a level of achievement that they are happy with, and tend to stay there. From the management viewpoint it becomes a problem when they reach that point, because you know you have something of quality that's moved and all of a sudden it levels out. You wonder, "How can I provoke this so it continues on the same trend?" I think that risk probably is an important thing that tends to be minimized. I mean management risks of accepting someone for a change in their role. You tend to perceive somebody as they have performed in the past, so you say, if he's a manufacturing man and he's done that for five years, then that's what I see him as everytime I see him—with a manufacturing frame around him and a label on it. But the risk thing I talk about is taking a man out of his role and putting him into another one which can build on his skills and maybe improve on some of his shortcomings, that will give more generalization or whatever. When I say risk, it's taking the risk of taking a known individual performing in his spot and satisfying my need as a manager, and then putting him in another spot where he may satisfy a greater need by giving him exposure. I then create for myself the threat of having to put somebody in his role, which is a new problem. I suspect that management people tend to be so cautious about covering all the risks that they don't really do enough to provoke the level of the high achiever to something even greater.

Covington: I think you are right. In fact, I like both of the points that you made. That first one is extremely important; where you have this person who is a high achiever and then he gets to a point where his performance either levels off, or in some cases even goes down.

Chilton: Sometimes just stating the words, "Why, you could be president," is just enough to plant a seed. You feel "if he thinks so, maybe I should think about it a little more."

Ends: It's fascinating in terms of expectations—of what it does for the person.

Chilton: As long as you don't create evidence of the Peter Principle.

Farrell: Or if it gets to the point that they're doing what they do so well that they can do it unconsciously; then they stop learning. You've got to give them something to do that they must strive for.

Kruel: I think most management people tend to be happy with that. The manager thinks, "I have the best of professional skills in every top slot and they're all happy and I'm happy"; and the organization stands still.

Page: And supervisors hire overqualified people to do the work and they end up with an unmotivated, unchallenged group of people.

Covington: Just send them into government!

four

Developing
Team-building Skills

OBJECTIVES

After reading Chapter Four you should be able to:

1. Describe the process by which interpersonal skills are developed.
2. Name the five major component skill areas that comprise the basic skills necessary in effective team building.

INTRODUCTION

Developing skill in building a team out of a collection of individuals is both one of the most exciting and one of the most difficult challenges faced by the young supervisor or manager. While there is no substitute for the team leader's detailed knowledge of the work in order to supervise, work knowledge alone does not make a good supervisor or team leader. Many outstanding engineers, for example, make very poor team leaders. The missing ingredient is skill in team building. As you might suspect, a large part of the component skills in team building are interpersonal skills. While some fortunate individuals seem to have an almost instinctive flair for team building, most people have to work hard at developing that skill.

Opportunities for developing team-building skills abound. Any group of people who must work together to accomplish a group task or goal provides an opportunity to develop team leadership skills. Even the family setting provides many opportunities for development of skill. For example, the family picnic or vacation, yard clean-up or landscaping, spring house cleaning or remodelling, and garage sales are a few possible family-team tasks. Schools also provide a wealth of opportunities to develop team-building skills, not only the athletic teams, but every hobby club or special interest group. Every special event provides opportunity to develop team-building skills. Most churches provide many opportunities, as do social organizations such as the Scouts, YMCA, and a host of others. A wide range of volunteer organizations sponsor fund-raising activities, get-out-the-vote drives, and save the environment campaigns, all of which provide opportunities to develop team-building skills. Finally, many business organizations provide such opportunities to their employees by recruiting volunteers for this special drive or that special task force in order to help meet their social obligations to the community. It is apparent that there is no shortage of opportunities to learn these skills, but even if you have not availed yourself of any of these, all is not lost. It is never too late to develop new skills or improve old ones.

Lovin and Casstevens have pointed out that skills are learned by doing. But what is the process by which one learns complex skills such as team building? First, let us define what we mean by skill. For our purposes we will define a *skill* as the dynamic process by which knowledge, experience, and ability are blended and applied in real-world situations to produce some desired result. The essence of the skill we are concerned with is the ability to influence the behavior of others in a special way. When others respond in the desired way, we say the person is skillful. If they respond in some way other than intended, we say the person lacks skill in influencing others. Yet some people seem never to develop such skills. Surely it is not that they do not wish to be able to influence the behavior of others. Influencing others is perhaps the principal and most natural activity of humankind. No, somehow they have not learned how to develop interpersonal skills. Perhaps we can better understand the development of skills by first examining how skill acquisition can be inhibited. The simplified diagram in Figure 4-1 shows one common way in which skill development is blocked.

To understand the process let's follow through the diagram with a simple example. Suppose you are with a group of people who are discussing how they might go about starting a Rock Hound Club. You feel they are just floundering around and are anxious to get them organized. You have mostly been listening and feel it is time you participated anyway. You sincerely want to be helpful. You jump up to the blackboard and say, "We're just wasting a lot of time. Let's get organized. First we need to divide up the tasks and give everyone an assignment, then we can get out of here." But the others do not respond as you intended. Instead they look at you with irritation and perhaps mutter comments like "Sit down," or "Get lost," or "Who invited him?" Your own reaction may be, "Gosh, I bombed out again. I guess I'm not cut out to be a leader." Or you may conclude that the group members are too stupid to know they need a leader. In either case, you have done nothing to develop skill. By blaming yourself for not being a leader, or blaming others for not following, you have probably perpetuated your ineffective skills, because you never questioned them. You assumed your "reading," or perception, of the situation was correct and you assumed that your behavior was correct for the situation as you saw it. Therefore the conclusion must be either that "I am not O.K." or "They are not O.K." or maybe both. You have reinforced your feeling that you are not a leader and/or you may have reinforced your feeling that other people are dumb, but you have learned nothing to increase your own effectiveness in influencing the behavior of others. In fact, if you have had similar results often in the past, you may have convinced yourself that it is impossible for you to lead others. The basic problem is that the interaction process as shown in Figure 4-1 is static rather than dynamic. It does not provide for change or learning. In fact, the confirmation loop shown

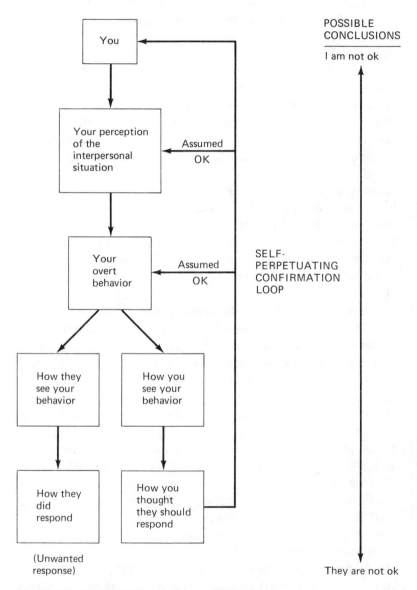

Figure 4-1. How Skill Development Can Be Prevented

serves only to perpetuate ineffective behavior. What is needed is a dynamic process that provides feedback such as that shown in Figure 4-2.

Using the same scenario presented in Figure 4-1, Figure 4-2 indicates how the process differs when one tries to learn from experience. Note first that the self-perpetuating confirmation loop has been omitted—it merely confirmed your ineffective behavior. Instead, the process is made dynamic by introduction of a feedback loop. The feedback loop tells you whether you are off target. Note that information from the unwanted response of others is used to trigger evaluation of both your reading of the situation and your behavior, which followed from it. In other words, when the response of others is different from what you anticipated, in effect you must ask yourself three questions. First, did I read the situation incorrectly? Second, was the nature of my participation inept, abrasive, or in some other way unskilled? Third, are they seeing my behavior different from the way I do? Notice that the conclusions drawn in this case are not judgments of either you or they. Instead, since you did not get the results you wanted, you are reassessing your skills for influencing others. Because all skills have both a perceptual and an action component, you question both aspects. They are distinctly different subskills which, for learning purposes, need to be examined separately. But because you behaved appropriately as you perceived the situation, how do you decide whether the action taken or the perception which led to it was off target?

One way out of the dilemma results from the fact that others respond to your behavior as *they* see it, not as *you* see it. If they had seen your behavior in the same way you saw it, they probably would have responded as you wanted them to. As a consequence, if you are to develop skill in influencing the responses of others, you must somehow discover how your behavior appears to others. Then you will be in a better position to learn how to get the responses you want. The ulti-

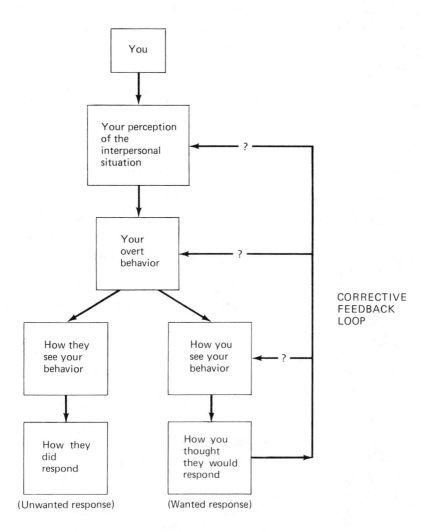

POSSIBLE CONCLUSIONS

1. I may be reading the situation wrong.
2. My behavior may have been inappropriate or unskilled.
3. They see my behavior different from the way I do.

Figure 4-2. How Interpersonal Skills Are Developed

mate goal is to learn to correctly read the continuous feedback provided by those with whom you may be interacting. The value of constant feedback, of course, is that it lets you know immediately when your behavior is generating unwanted responses in others. Then you can modify your participation. With sufficient skill, you can sense the off-target condition and modify your approach before you have reached the point of no return.

Once you have decided that either your perceptual skills or your interactive skills are not effective in producing the results you want, then you must embark on the discovery of more effective methods. Once found, it requires a great deal of practice before you can expect to become truly skillful in their use. This is where a good coach can be of great help. A coach can help you make sure that you are practicing the right things. Figure 4-3 shows how a coach can speed up skill development by providing feedback and by suggesting alternative ways of looking at things and different behavioral approaches.

As shown in Figure 4-3, a coach can help you learn to read interpersonal situations more accurately and help you improve the effectiveness of your ways of interacting with others. This includes such things as the way you express yourself, habits and mannerisms, timing, flexibility, and assertiveness, to name a few. From the observer's vantage point, the coach can also help you understand how others see your behavior. Finally, the coach can help you learn to read the responses of others more accurately.

Few people can afford the luxury of a professional coach. Most people have discovered that good coaching is readily available from a wide range of people with whom they usually interact—simply for the asking. The trick is to identify those people you know and respect who seem to be particularly adept at some aspect of interpersonal behavior. For example, if you see someone who is adept at sensing the group's feel-

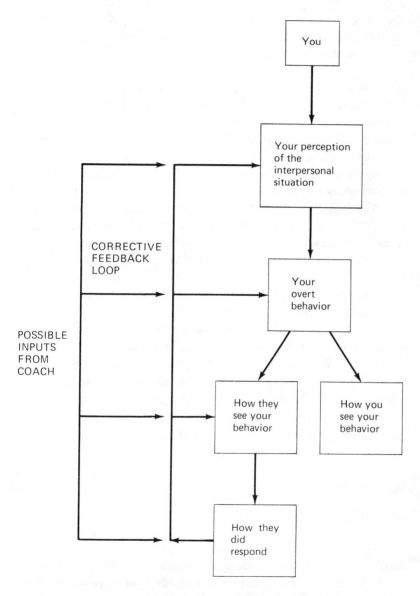

Figure 4-3. How a Coach Can Help Speed Skill Development

ings or its readiness to come to a decision, ask that person to help you learn to do it. Most people will be eager to help you. You might find another person who seems to have the knack for getting others involved in the group task. Observe those behavioral techniques and compare them to your own. You might try someone else's techniques on your own, or you might ask the other person to help you learn them. Thus, instead of a single coach, you may have many different coaches helping you develop your interpersonal skills. This approach gives *you* the job of head coach, a role you must assume sooner or later anyway.

Whether you take courses in leadership training, or receive guidance from one or more coaches, or simply try to do it all by yourself, the *process* of learning interpersonal skills is much the same. It is a process of training yourself to learn from your own experience in interpersonal situations. You will learn faster if you are careful to follow the rules for adult learning discussed in Chapter Three. Review them if necessary.

The general process of skill development we have discussed applies to all of the component skills needed to develop a group of individuals into an effective work team. Five major component skill areas comprise the basic skills necessary in effective team building. The five skill areas are (1) self-understanding, (2) understanding individual team members, (3) understanding the team, (4) planning team performance, and (5) developing team communication.

SELF-UNDERSTANDING

Skill in understanding one's self begins with self-assessment, a sort of inventory of your current assets and liabilities as a person and as a potential team leader. That information, important as it is to you, merely provides the starting point for development of skill in understanding yourself. The reason for this is that as you learn and grow, you are forever changing in significant ways. Thus even a very thorough assessment of yourself at some point in your life can be useful information only at that point in time. It gradually becomes obsolete information as you gain new experience, as you learn, and as you grow. Therefore, to understand oneself means that one must develop a dynamic, lifelong process that provides for frequent self-reassessment. One of the most effective ways to do this is by developing skill in reading the continuous feedback provided by your daily interaction with others. Such information enables you to identify areas of your own performance where your knowledge or skill is weak. It also enables you to evaluate the success of your experimenting with new techniques to improve your effectiveness as a team leader.

In one sense, developing interpersonal skills is a matter of learning how to lift yourself up by your own bootstraps. The key to the process is learning to read the feedback from each part of your performance, then changing your performance the next time to improve the results. Since performance is usually an ongoing sequence of activity made up of many distinct actions, feedback is continuous. The trick is to learn how to read it continuously and to respond to it continuously. This means, of course, that you must have a clear idea of the kind of results you are trying to achieve. In the area of interpersonal skills, you are trying to influence the perceptions, the feelings, and the behavior of other people. Therefore, how they respond to your attempts to influence them can provide much of the feedback you need, if only you can learn to read it.

For the purpose of developing team-building skills we are concerned with six aspects of skill in self-understanding: (1) how you relate to others; (2) your impact on others;

(3) your strengths; (4) how you use your strengths; (5) your weaknesses; and (6) how you cope with your weaknesses.

How Do You Relate to Others?

Much of a team leader's influence is affected through face-to-face interaction with team members. Therefore you might begin your self-assessment by asking yourself how you generally interact with or relate to others in groups in work or social situations. Are you the initiator who tries to get others to join with you in doing things? Or do you usually wait for others to invite you to join in? Do you insist on always being a Chief, or do you prefer the role of Indian? Do you express warmth and friendliness toward others? Do you like others to express warmth toward you?

An organized way of getting answers to such questions was developed by W. C. Schutz. It consists of a self-description inventory known as FIRO-B (*F*undamental *I*nterpersonal *R*elations *I*nventory-*B*ehavioral). The inventory helps you assess your behavior *as you see it* with respect to three dimensions. The first dimension is labeled *inclusion*, which deals with the need to associate and interact with others. The second dimension is labeled *control* and assesses your need for dominance or control in your relations with others. The third dimension, *affection*, assesses your need for warmth and friendliness in your interpersonal relations. Two aspects of your behavior in each dimension are examined. The first is the behavior you see yourself as expressing toward others; that is, the behavior you initiate. The other aspect is the behavior you want others to express toward you; that is, the behavior in others to which you will probably respond favorably. This scheme results in six scales which can be represented as shown in Table 4-1.

An inventory such as FIRO-B will give you a pretty good

Table 4-1. FIRO–B Scale Measurements

	Inclusion	*Control*	*Affection*
Expressed	Amount of including behavior you express toward others	Amount of controlling behavior you express toward others	Amount of affection you express toward others
Wanted	Amount of including behavior you want others to express toward you	Amount of controlling behavior you want others to express toward you	Amount of affection you want others to express toward you

idea of *how you see yourself* in your relations with others. The question that then arises is: Are you assessing yourself correctly? After all, other people react to your behavior as it appears to them, not as it appears to you. As a consequence, to develop skill in self-assessment of your behavior you need some source of data other than your own opinion. Fortunately your behavior has been observed, experienced, and reacted to by others who have known you for some time. So the opportunity exists for comparing your estimate of your behavior with their assessments of your behavior. The comparison will give you a pretty good idea of just how accurate your self-assessment of your own behavior is. In other words, skill in assessing your own behavior begins with trying to get some idea of how others see your behavior, then trying to adjust your self-perceptions to match.

What Is Your Impact on Others?

Your opinion of your own behavior in relation to others on the inclusion, control, and affection dimensions is of little value unless it approximates the way others see you. The simplest way to begin to discover your impact on others is to ask a number of classmates you have worked with to describe your behavior using the FIRO-B or a similar inventory. Since different people will probably have somewhat different assessments of your behavior, averaging their scores should give you a pretty good idea of how others see you. While an inventory such as FIRO-B by no means describes your *total* impact on others, it does provide a good starting point. The information derived by comparing your own scores with the average scores of those who use it to describe your behavior can be used in several ways. The first way is to examine the possible causes of any major differences. For example, if you see yourself as expressing more including behavior than others see you expressing, what might account for the difference? Are you perhaps thinking of how you behave when you are with close friends? It is common for most of us to behave quite differently when with those we know very well. Or are you perhaps thinking of your behavior among a group

Table 4-2. Self-Rating of Team Leader Skills

Rate yourself on a scale of one to five on each of the skill areas below, using the following rating scores:

RATING SCALE

1—considerably below average
2—somewhat below average
3—about average
4—somewhat above average
5—considerably above average

RATING	*SKILL AREA*
_____	Communication skills
_____	Planning skills
_____	Organizing skills
_____	Coaching skills
_____	Persuasive skills
_____	Negotiating skills

---

of intimates as the "real" you? This possibility can be checked out by asking intimate friends to describe your behavior as they see it on the inventory.

Is their description closer to your own perception than that of your classmates? If so, then you may have to re-examine your assessment of how you behave in groups that are not made up of close friends. The most important thing to keep in mind when doing so is that the question of who is right and who is wrong is never the issue. The whole purpose is to find out how others see your behavior so that you can adjust your own understanding. If you know how others see your behavior, then you can better understand why they respond to you the way they do.

What Are Your Strengths?

An important aspect of developing skill in self-under-standing is identifying your strengths. What sorts of things can you do well? What have you got going for you as a potential team leader? The list of team leader skills in Table 4-2 will help you assess your strengths as well as your weaknesses. In order to rate yourself on the skills listed in Table 4-2, think of how you have performed in each of the skill areas compared to the way you feel most of your peers perform in various work groups, whether it be in the classroom, in sports, or on the job. Try to compare yourself with the average, neither the best nor the worst. But first let us briefly examine each of the skill areas so you have a pretty good idea of just what we are concerned with in each skill area.

Communication Skills

Above all the team leader must be an effective communicator. This person must be able to get ideas across clearly not only to team members but to many others as well. He or she must be able to communicate well with a wide variety of people on a one-to-one basis. But it is even more important that a leader develop considerable skill in communicating to groups of people. Such a person is often called on to make formal presentations to organizational superiors or to another group, to lead his or her own group in discussions, and to frequently address the team to explain the task or to give them feedback. Remember, communication is the only medium by which any person influences the perception, the feelings, and the behavior of others.

Planning Skills

An effective team leader must have not only a very clear idea of the goal, but also a clear understanding of what must be done to get there. The effective leader must be able to plan all the activities it will take to reach the goal. He or she must also be able to plan the sequence in which the activities must occur. In other words, the team leader must be able to develop a road map that describes how to get the team from their starting point to where they want to go—in an organized fashion. The leader must be able to communicate the plans so everyone understands clearly.

Organizing Skills

Planning is a way of organizing the work before actually starting it and is one kind of organizing skill. However, skill in organizing the team members is a related but different kind of skill. It involves the leadership skill of matching the individual team members and their abilities and needs to the various tasks that must be done. Part of the team leader's job is making sure that each team member has a clear idea of what is expected from each, when it is expected, and how he or she is expected to work in coordination with other team members. The leader must also make sure that the work load is distributed fairly so that no one has either too much or too little to do. In addition, he or she must make sure that help, including coaching, is available when a team member needs it.

Coaching Skills

Coaching skills include being able to demonstrate to a team member exactly how to go about performing a specific task. It requires that the leader be able to help set performance goals and teach the member how to measure progress toward the goals. It also means that the leader must help the member diagnose performance problems and correct errors. Finally, it includes skill in providing feedback on performance in a way that encourages the person to try harder.

Persuasive Skills

Under this general heading are the skills required in selling, convincing, inspiring, and encouraging others. All involve the ability to capture other people's imaginations, to create in their minds a realization that some of their desires are within reach if they will but take the required action or expend the necessary effort. The capacity for empathy, the ability to put yourself in the other person's shoes, is a vital ingredient in the persuasive skills.

Negotiating Skills

The effective team leader often finds considerable use for negotiating skills. First of all, he or she may have to negotiate with each team member regarding the role each will take in the group task. The team leader typically negotiates schedules. This person may be expected to negotiate the price for team performance, whether it is paid in dollars or in some other kind of recognition. The leader may have to negotiate for a meeting place, for supplies used, for a work or practice

place, and for a host of other things. Success in these negotiations can have a very strong effect on the morale of the team.
As a consequence it is important that the leader have negotiating skill sufficient to make sure that the team gets at least
their share of the rewards, conveniences, and resources available.

Now, with these brief descriptions in mind, turn back to
Table 4-2 and rate yourself after carefully thinking through
how well you perform in each area compared to your peers.

As a rule of thumb, you can consider as one of your
strengths any skill on which you rated yourself either 4 or 5.
You might also wish to have some acquaintances who have
worked with you rate you on the same scale. This will provide you with additional data on how others see you. It will
also give you an opportunity to check your self-perceptions.

How Do You Use Your Strengths?

After identifying your strengths, the next question is:
How do you use them? It has been said that people are more
apt to get in trouble because of their strengths than because
of their weaknesses. The reason for this is that people have a
tendency to overdo those things they do well simply because
they enjoy the satisfaction of successful performance. The
result is too much of a good thing. The team leader who excels at planning may spend too much time planning, and not
enough time doing. The leader who excels in selling may get
carried away and sell things the team cannot deliver. Or the
team leader who enjoys and excels at coaching may neglect
some other leadership duties. In other words, there is a tendency to use our strengths too much or to use them inappro-
priately. For example, a leader may try to rely on coaching

skill where organizing skill is required. While most people build on their existing skills, their misuse reduces the team leader's effectiveness. Even worse, it prevents the leader from developing the skills in which he or she is weak. To increase our team-development skills you must know not only your strengths, but also your weaknesses.

What Are Your Weaknesses?

In rating yourself on Table 4-2 you identified not only your strengths, but also the skill areas in which you are weak. These are the skill areas where you gave yourself (or your acquaintances scored you) a 1 or a 2. Your overall effectiveness as a team leader will be limited by these weak areas. Since skills are learned by doing, the way to overcome deficiencies is obvious: Seek opportunities to practice, and search out the best coach you can find.

How Do You Cope with Your Weaknesses?

There are several ways of coping with weaknesses in skill areas. One is to try to substitute a strength. That approach might work sometimes, but it also can reduce your motivation for developing skill in areas in which you are weak. Another common way of coping with skill deficiencies is simply to get someone who has the necessary skill to perform that part of your leadership role for you. Such delegation is quite common in large organizations; for example, the planning function may be delegated to a group of specialists. The problem with delegation is that while a leader can delegate authority to perform part of the managing job, that person can never delegate the *responsibility* to another. Responsibility for the performance of others is inherent in the manager's or team leader's role, and there is no way that person can escape it and remain a leader. Consequently, those who aspire to leadership must be willing to pay the price of learning the necessary team leader skills. Without them the leader endangers his or her own position, by having to rely on others to help perform special leadership tasks.

UNDERSTANDING INDIVIDUAL TEAM MEMBERS

One of the keys to successful team development and leadership is through understanding each of your team members as individuals. Even though they are willing to work together toward a common goal, each is also trying to satisfy personal needs and goals. Each has a private value system that is most important. Each has distinctive motivational patterns, an individual self-concept, unique prior experiences, and his or her own special perception of you and your role as team leader. As a consequence, the effective team leader must learn what these differences are and somehow take them into account when developing the team. What this means is that the team leader must invest a considerable amount of time, initially, getting to know the individual members of the team. Developing skill in understanding your team members as individuals begins with gaining a clear idea of the kinds of things that influence people's behavior, then learning how to acquire that knowledge about each person. Because every person is a living, growing, changing organism, understanding another calls for the development of your capacity for empathy. In simplest terms, *empathy* is the ability to put yourself in someone else's shoes, so to speak. If you can understand where the other person is coming from, you can interact effectively. In order to develop empathic skill, one begins by learning as much as one can about each team member. A good place to start is with the person's value system and personal goals.

Value Systems and Personal Goals

The values and personal goals that the team leader must understand are those that are related to the team task. For example, what does the team member hope to get out of participating in the team activity? What is important to the team member? Is he or she seeking companionship? recognition? Is the member hoping to develop some skill or learn better ways of doing things? Is this person looking for acceptance and friendship? trying to gain experience? trying to prove something to himself or herself or to others? Or is the person a member only because someone has to be, because somebody assigned him or her to your team? Does the member really know what he or she wants to get out of participation? Is he or she willing to work hard to attain those goals or merely looking for a free ride?

The simplest way to discover such things is simply to ask. While you may get some "socially acceptable" answers rather than the pure truth, you can also get a pretty good idea of what a member wants in return for participation. Once you identify those wants, you must then evaluate whether the team activity can provide it. Will the nature of the task and the type of interaction among team members permit an individual member to achieve personal goals if all goes well? If not, that fact should be made known to the member and discussed. The potential rewards and satisfactions your specific team can provide, and what it cannot provide, should be clearly understood by both you and every other team member at the outset. This can prevent team members from suddenly turning off when they realize that their personal goals are not going to be met by the team activity. In such situations, team members may feel that they have been used, or conned, by the team leader.

Motivational Patterns

Skill in understanding your team members also requires that you understand something about the motivational patterns of each of them. The motivational patterns of individuals are much more difficult to identify than are their values and personal goals. As Gellerman has said, "The first and most important thing to be said about motives is that everybody has a lot of them and that nobody has quite the same mixture as anyone else." However true that may be, Maslow has provided several simplifying concepts that aid in understanding motivation.

We may define *motivation* as behavior instigated by needs and directed toward the goals that will satisfy those needs. Maslow has classified all human needs into five basic categories:

1. Physiological needs; e.g., thirst, hunger, sex.
2. Safety needs; e.g., security and freedom from psychological or physical attack.
3. A need to belong; e.g., love, friendship, affection.
4. The need for esteem; e.g., self-respect and the respect of others.
5. The need for self-actualization; e.g., growth and self-fulfillment.

Maslow has pointed out that lower needs are usually given priority; for example, when extremely hungry, a person will usually stop whatever she or he is doing and take time to satisfy the hunger need. Once the need is satisfied, it loses its motivating force and the person returns to the original behavior which was directed toward satisfying some higher-order need such as the need for esteem. Most needs cannot be satisfied as simply and quickly as the physiological needs. The need for esteem, for example, often requires much more persistent behavior over a considerable period of time in order to reach a state of satisfaction. For example, you may work very hard for four years to satisfy your need for esteem by earning your college diploma. But as Sigmund Freud once pointed out, all behavior is overdetermined. By that he meant that in a specific behavioral sequence, people are always trying to satisfy several needs at the same time. For instance, a person working toward a college diploma may be satisfying other needs for security, for belongingness, and for esteem by that course of action as well. Given a choice, most people will select a course of action that enables them to satisfy several needs at the same time.

Another characteristic of motivation is that a variety of specific goals may satisfy the underlying need. For example, how many ways can you think of that would help satisfy your need for the esteem of others? The list is endless. As a consequence, to understand the motivational patterns of others, the team leader must learn to evaluate specific goals team members may set for themselves in terms of the basic need the person is trying to satisfy. In the work environment, it is reasonably safe to assume that the need for esteem is seldom met to the individual's satisfaction. If someone clearly sees an opportunity to help satisfy that need by participating in team activity, he or she will generally jump at the chance.

As a rule, people who are regarded as "loners" have a low need for belongingness, with respect to their co-workers, and do not make good team members. Careful observation of loners often reveals that they have an extremely high need to be independent. They meet their need for self-esteem by being independent, and they often take great pride in their independence. Since the essence of teamwork is acceptance of the interdependence of team members on each other to get the job done, the true loner is usually more trouble than he or she is worth.

Developing skill in understanding the motivational patterns of others thus boils down to careful observation of their behavior. By noting what seems to turn them on, what seems to turn them off, what kind of questions they ask, how they respond to ideas, to suggestions, and to the behavior of others all provide clues as to the dominant needs they are trying to satisfy. Those who are trying to satisfy their esteem needs by high achievement, for example, will typically work much harder when criticized than when praised. On the other hand, those who are trying to fulfill their need for belongingness by team activity will usually work much harder when praised than when criticized. The normal give and take of a working group usually provides opportunity for the careful observer to discern such patterns. Individual coaching sessions also provide an opportunity. This is especially so if the team leader gives the members a chance to discuss and evaluate their own performance and establish their own performance-improvement goals. It should be noted that trying to understand motivational patterns of others is perhaps the most difficult and most frustrating task of the team leader. It is a difficult skill to acquire, but is well worth the effort. It can pay off handsomely in greater effectiveness.

Self-concepts

Any person's self-concept is of course related to that person's values, goals, needs, and motivational patterns. These all provide clues as to how one sees oneself. As discussed in Chapter Three, much of anyone's behavior is aimed at actualizing the self-concept—making it real—at least in one's own mind. Skill in sensing or understanding another's self-concept, then, is developed by inferring from a person's behavior just what kind of self-image he or she holds dear.

For purposes of team building, one of the most significant ways in which people perceive themselves is with respect to their ability to get what they want out of life. James and Jongeward, in *Born to Win*, use the terms "winners" and "losers" to describe two opposite sets of self-concepts which have a very great impact on the behavior of the people who hold them. Fortunately, most people are neither total losers nor total winners. Most people are winners in some areas of their lives, while they are losers in others. Everyone has read of outstanding winners in the science, business, political, or entertainment fields who have been notorious losers in other areas of their lives.

Because most people have a mixture of winner and loser self-images, the skill a team leader must develop is to discover the team members' self-concepts with respect to the team activity. For example, many people have loser self-concepts regarding their ability to function as salespeople. Since winner and loser self-concepts regarding an area of performance tend to become self-fulfilling prophecies, the importance to the team leader is obvious. Helping losers become winners is a job for a skilled psychotherapist, not for a team leader. The team leader will do well to develop the skill required to detect winner and loser self-concepts with respect to the task at hand.

What are some of the behavioral clues that indicate winner or loser self-concepts with respect to group roles? Perhaps the simplest clue is whether the team member expresses a positive or a negative attitude toward the task at hand. The person with winner self-concepts will see the task as a challenge, as an opportunity to satisfy some needs, as a chance to demonstrate competence or to acquire new competence. In other words, a winner will show enthusiasm for the task. He or she may eagerly seek the assignment. On the other hand, a person with loser self-concepts concerning the task will bring up all the things that might go wrong. The loser sees the task not as an opportunity for success, but as an opportunity for failure. A loser will rarely volunteer unless pushed into it by pressure from the group or the team leader. If assigned such a task, he or she will probably expend more effort on self-protection than on getting the job done.

As with development of all interpersonal skills, the key is training yourself to read the communication and feedback that is constantly available to the team leader in the work situation.

Prior Experience

Another important aspect of developing skill in understanding your individual team members involves learning about related past experiences they may have had. Have they had any experience with similar activities? If not, do they really understand what is expected of them? Will they have to learn everything from scratch? If so, who will be able to teach them? If they have had experience at similar activities, what was their role? Were they Chief or Indian? Was the experience a satisfying one? Did the individual learn anything that may be of value in the current endeavor? If the previous experience was not satisfying, why is the individual participating this time? What special skills does the person bring to the team that may make him or her especially valuable? How did the person get along with other team members? With the team leader?

Answers to questions like these will help the team leader develop skill in understanding team members. Answers to many of them can be had merely for the asking. Answers to others will have to be pieced together from many bits and pieces of data. But in any case, the more you know about the nature of the team members' related prior experiences, the more effectively you can deal with them.

How They See You

In the first section of this chapter we discussed the development of skill in understanding yourself. One aspect of that skill involved learning to see how you come across to others by the way they respond to you. Once a climate of openness, honesty, and trust have been established, you can simply ask them how they see you, or sense it in the everyday give and take of the work situation. Initially you have little data to work with. Yet the early stages of your relationship can be very critical. A thoughtless word or action may be used to excite team members' fears or raise their anxiety. What is especially important is how they see your role as team leader and how they see you fitting into that role. On the one hand, some team members may see the leadership role as calling for a strong, dictatorial type of leader. Another may feel the role calls for a more democratic leader. Some will have no idea of the style of leadership best suited to the task situation. But all of them will be continuously evaluating your style of leadership, as they see it, against their expectations of the role. Remember, they will respond to you as they see you, in the role in which they individually have cast you in their own minds, not necessarily in the way you see yourself.

The kinds of questions you should try to answer with respect to team members, as individuals, are the following. Are they afraid of me? Do they respect me? How much help do they expect me to give them? Do they see me as an autocrat? Do they seem to feel they have a special relationship with me? Do they see me as an antagonist? Do they see me as a winner or as a loser? Do they see me as fair or unfair in my dealings with them? Do they see me as helpful? as too critical? as competent or incompetent? as friendly or unfriendly? as indifferent?

The purpose in trying to discover how various team members see you is fairly obvious. It tells you something about the kind of interpersonal obstacles you will have to overcome to be effective in your role as a team leader. It provides some clues about how to approach your coaching tasks with each individual. And it will also tell you something about how others see you and respond to your behavior, your attitudes, and your habits and mannerisms. The person who would lead others must in many ways be the most sensitive, the most flexible, and the most adaptable member of the team.

UNDERSTANDING YOUR TEAM

Understanding your team as a unit is a quite different skill from the skill of understanding the individual team members. Understanding your team as a unit means trying to understand what this particular combination of individuals is capable of doing on a team task. Performance capability of a group is not the same as the sum of all the abilities of the individual members of the group. Team performance depends on how the pluses and minuses of the team members interact to reinforce or cancel out each other. In other words, the whole may be *greater* than the sum of its parts; it may also be *less* than the sum of its parts. To help understand the reasons for this, let's examine some of the main factors you must take into account to develop skill in understanding your team as a team. We will confine our discussion to seven important aspects: (1) the experience and capability mix; (2) existing interpersonal relationships among team members; (3) awareness of interdependence; (4) the quality of intergroup communication; (5) group cohesiveness; (6) group morale; (7) group perception of your leadership role.

The Experience and Capability Mix of Your Team

As a group, what kinds of experience and ability can be counted among the team's total resources that will help it get the job done? Does it include at least some prior experience in each of the various tasks that will have to be performed? For example, if the team project requires telephone solicitation or door-to-door selling, does the team actually possess any members with first-hand experience at such tasks? If so, was it a successful experience? Do the members who have had successful experience have the skill and willingness to train other team members if necessary? Or, if the team does not possess the necessary experience or skill, how can you as team leader provide it? One way is to train them yourself, if you have the skill. Another is to find someone with the necessary skill to coach your team members in doing those jobs for which neither you nor they have sufficient skill to ensure success.

The effective team leader does not make assumptions about the experience and ability of a team. He or she will very carefully evaluate the various tasks that must be done, estimate the level of experience and skill required for each, and then evaluate the team. The manager/leader does this because she or he understands the importance of success to building a strong team and is therefore very careful to assure that the team either possesses the necessary experience and ability for the job at hand or will be able to acquire it very early in the game. The goal is to provide a steady stream of small successes for each team member and for the team as a whole as it moves toward its goal.

It is not wise for the leader of an untried team to rely completely on team members' assessments of their own abilities. The leader must form his or her own assessments from observing the team members perform. Some will tend to overstate their abilities and prior experience, others will understate theirs. If the nature of the team project permits, it is very helpful to hold dry runs or rehearsals. Role playing is a very good technique that the team leader can use to evaluate just how good team members are where interpersonal skills such as selling are required. If the task calls for dealing with the public in a selling role, members can take turns playing customer and salesperson roles, for example. The most experienced salesperson on the team can then serve as coach.

For technical skills, such as bookkeeping or carpentry, for example, there is only one safe way for the team leader to assess the team's capability. That is by watching the actual performance, or looking at the product. This means, of course, that the team leader must have sufficient technical knowledge in the required areas so that he or she can tell good performance from bad. If the leader does not possess such knowledge, then he or she must rely on the judgment of team members and hope for the best, or find an expert with whom to consult.

In the final analysis, the team leader must eventually put the team to the test to see what abilities they actually bring to bear on the task. Again, the initial tests should be fairly easy ones, and, if possible, not terribly important ones. The reason for this is that if the leader has misjudged the abilities of the team members, the failures will be small ones and the situation can be corrected before too much is lost.

Existing Interpersonal Relationships

Close friendships or animosity between two or more people may exist due to previous experience before they joined your team. Such relationships can create problems in team development. They often result in subgroups within the team. Close friends may be unwilling to work on two-person tasks with anyone but each other. Or they may tend to ignore the third person on a three-person task, thus creating hard feelings. Pre-existing animosities can split a group into warring subgroups or keep it from ever developing into a productive team.

It is quite normal for team members to develop preferences; they will like some members more than others. The team leader should try to recognize such preferences and take them into account whenever the nature of the task permits it and when it does not interfere with getting the job done. Animosity, on the other hand, is quite another problem. Sooner or later, if it is allowed to continue, it will disrupt group performance. If the ill feeling between two team members is the result of a prior conflict, the team leader must face up to it as soon as he or she discovers it. The simplest approach is to get together with both involved members and ask them whether they will be able to work together. If one feels he or she cannot work with the other, then at least one and maybe both should be dismissed from the team.

Being Aware of Interdependence

One of the critical ingredients in successful team performance is an awareness on the part of each team member that he or she needs the other members. Each has a part to play in reaching the team goal. No one team member can win the game alone. When the team members with the more glamorous assignments start thinking of themselves as "stars", trouble is sure to follow. Successful team developers make a special point of reinforcing the awareness of interdependence among team members. They may do this by rotating assignments whenever possible. Or they may make a point of emphasizing how important each person's performance is to the total effort required to reach the goal. Even Wilt (the Stilt) Chamberlain finally discovered that he could not win a basketball game by himself; it took all five players.

Evaluating Intergroup Communication

How and what do the team members communicate to one another? The way team members talk to each other can reveal much about their attitudes toward each other. Members of effective teams usually have considerable respect for their teammates. This is revealed in discussions by showing consideration for the viewpoint of the others, for the others' feelings, and so on. Is information exchanged freely and openly? Or is communication guarded and limited entirely to talk about the job? Do team members seem to withhold useful information from each other? What is the general tenor of the communication? Does it reflect optimism or pessimism about the task or the group goal? All of these are things the successful team leader learns to listen for because they can tell much about the cohesiveness and the morale of a team at any point in time. This permits the leader to correct the situation before it gets out of hand.

Evaluating Team Cohesiveness

Cohesiveness refers to the attraction members have for each other. If they like to be together and work together as a group, and resist any effort to divide them into several distinct groups, then we say the team is cohesive. They tend to stick together. The reason groups develop cohesiveness is because they help satisfy each member's needs. All members expect to meet some of their needs for self-esteem, and the esteem of others, by participating on a winning team. Yet if they are aware of their interdependence on the others to help reach the team goal, they begin to feel warm and friendly toward those who are helping them to satisfy their own needs. Because all friendships are based on mutual need satisfaction of some sort, cohesiveness indicates that the teammates feel they are benefitting from continuing to work together. On the other hand, a lack of cohesiveness can mean either that the members do not know each other very well or that they see no opportunity for mutual need satisfaction. This may be due to a lack of respect, lack of trust, or animosities among the membership.

Evaluating Morale

Morale refers to the confidence a team has in its ability, as a team, to achieve difficult goals. It includes the will to win, but it also involves much more. For all team members to have confidence in the ability of the team means that each feels that all teammates have not only the necessary skills and abilities to do the job but also the will and the personal commitment to do their best in working together to achieve the goal. Each one can count on all the rest to do their best. Then, just as it does with the individual, this feeling of confidence and commitment tends to become a self-fulfilling prophecy. It is easy to see why team leaders are so concerned about morale.

Perhaps one of the best indicators of team morale is the enthusiasm the members show in performing their jobs. High morale and enthusiasm tend to go hand in hand. Another clue lies in the quality of group communication. High morale groups are quite open, friendly, honest, respectful, and generally positive in their communications with one another. Complaints about the performance of a fellow teammate are

rarely voiced. Instead, teammates are more interested in helping each other improve performance. High-morale teams
usually show a high degree of cohesiveness as well. Since they
are all working toward a common goal, and have learned to
count on one another, they usually develop a genuine liking
for their teammates. Morale, then, is a kind of overall indi-
cator of the extent to which a collection of individuals think
of themselves as a team and how well they think they can
perform as a team. Every successful team leader has learned
to become sensitive to all the bits and pieces of human behavior that indicate the condition of the team's morale.

How Team Members View the Leadership Role

    A final aspect of developing skill in understanding your
team involves assessing their perception of your leadership
role. Because most people have had some prior experience
with groups, nearly everyone will come into the group with
some idea of what the leader is supposed to do. Each has a
special version of what he or she expects of you in your role
as leader. Each is ready to judge your performance as leader
against those expectations. One member may expect you to
personally make all the assignments, issue orders, and make
all the decisions. Another may expect you to do nothing
more than the coordinating, record-keeping, and reporting
job. Another may expect you to spend all of your time coaching various team members. Obviously you cannot satisfy
everyone's initial expectations; furthermore, they probably
have not made them known to you. How can this role dilemma be resolved?
    The simplest way to deal with the definition of your role
as leader is by the process of role negotiation with your team
members. This is not a cop out. The responsibility for performance of the team and each member of it rests on you.

Your team members will share some of that responsibility, but you alone are held accountable. As a consequence, it is in your own best interest to have a very clear understanding between yourself and your team of just what they can expect of you as their leader. Open negotiation of your role will help set the pattern of openness and trust in the group. Even in organizations in which the leadership role is already defined by tradition or by job desciption, there are always many important aspects that are not spelled out in detail. In fact, the most important aspects are generally ignored entirely. The nature of the leader's personal interaction with the team is seldom mentioned.

The kinds of things that need to be negotiated are the extent of team participation in goal setting and decision making, the amount of coaching and other supervisory help the leader or other members will provide, how discipline will be handled if the occasion arises, how assignments will be made, what the standards of acceptable performance are, what the work loads will be, and how various emergencies will be dealt with. Briefly, it adds up to spelling out in open negotiation exactly what the team can expect from the leader and what the leader can expect from the team under the forseeable circumstances. It can save needless disappointment, argument, hostility, and inefficiency to clear the air with respect to your leadership role at the outset rather than waiting until problems arise.

PLANNING TEAM PERFORMANCE

Successful team performance is rarely an accident. Most often it is the result of careful planning. Planning provides a good opportunity to get the team members involved in the project early in the game. It helps them feel as though it is *their* project, rather than *your* project. However, team involvement in the planning process at the very beginning of a project can be a very frustrating and time consuming affair unless all the members have a great deal of experience. One way of saving time while still gaining the benefits of group involvement in the planning process is for you as the team leader to present a tentative plan for consideration. By outlining the general strategy you feel is right for the job at hand, you can often gain acceptance for the overall approach. If everyone agrees to the general approach, then the team members will have plenty of opportunity to become involved in the details of the planning which most directly affect them. But regardless of how it is done, there are five major aspects that should be addressed in planning team performance. These are (1) establishing team performance goals, (2) planning the work, (3) negotiating roles, (4) establishing performance criteria, and (5) planning performance feedback. Because most of these topics have already been discussed in the previous pages, a brief summary of the main points under each should suffice.

Establishing Team Performance Goals

The purpose for which the team was formed identifies the basic team goal; for example, raising funds for some charity. But the performance goal itself will often be part of the planning process. In the case of fund raising, for example, your team may agree to a performance goal of, say, $2,000 within a one-month period. A team performance goal, then, states how much, how many, how soon, or how well. It is a statement of what constitutes success in reaching the goal for which the team was formed. By being specific, it helps greatly in the planning process because it helps define the scope of the endeavor and forces more realistic planning. A manager who tells subordinate managers to reduce their costs 10 percent will probably get the 10 percent reduction asked for. But if she or he merely tells subordinates to reduce their costs as much as they can, there is no telling what the results may be.

Research has clearly demonstrated that the leader's performance goals for the team are of crucial importance. In high-performing groups the leader always expects more from the group than they initially believe they can deliver. The leader doesn't expect the impossible, but does expect a level of performance that will require members to stretch themselves a bit. Thus reaching the goal becomes something of a challenge, something the team will have to work hard to achieve. One of the main concerns of the leader in the performance goal-setting process, then, is to make sure the goal represents a reasonable challenge, neither too difficult nor too easy.

Planning the Work

Once the performance goals have been agreed on, all the various tasks that are required can be identified. This also offers an opportunity for team-member involvement. Again the team leader can save much time and still gain the benefits of team-member participation by identifying the various functions that must be provided by the team; for example, advertising, purchasing, scheduling, bookkeeping, and so forth, depending on the nature of the team endeavor. Once the functions have been listed, the specific tasks to be performed under each function can be more easily identified. One advantage of team involvement in planning the work is that it enables each member to get a pretty good idea of what is required and what will be expected of the person performing a specific task. This will help set the stage for the next step in planning team performance: negotiating roles.

Negotiating Roles

Once all concerned have a pretty good idea of what work the team must do to reach its goals, the specific tasks each member will perform can then be negotiated. While the term *negotiation* may sound a bit formal and legalistic, it is used to emphasize the idea of making sure that there is clear agreement and understanding of what each person expects of the others and in turn what others can expect of them. Without a clear agreement of what and how each will contribute, commitment to the team project is of little value because no one knows just what any team member is actually committed to.

Establishing Performance Criteria

Since all the separate tasks that make up the team project are interdependent, it follows that how well any one task is done will influence overall team performance. As a consequence, it is necessary to establish performance standards for each task. Usually these take the form of minimum performance standards that can be tolerated without jeopardizing the team performance goals. If the team member feels it is impossible to meet the standards, then some form of assistance can be planned for, or the work load redistributed. To prevent disastrous surprises—such as discovering that a team member who agreed to sell two hundred tickets for the Hobby Fair actually managed to sell only ten—some form of performance feedback should be planned.

Planning Performance Feedback

Two kinds of performance feedback should be provided. First, individual team members should be asked to report progress on their various tasks to the team leader. These reports should be frequent enough so the team leader can provide assistance or take some other action if all is not going well—before it is too late. The second kind of feedback is from the team leader to the team as a whole, and to the various team members individually, on how they are doing. While each may have a pretty good idea of whether he or she is meeting specific task-performance goals, feedback from the leader to that effect is always welcome. But equally important is feedback from the leader on how the team as a whole is progressing. This kind of feedback helps build morale and develop cohesiveness. It provides the individual team member with reassurance that the effort is worthwhile and that the team is beginning to function like a team should, with everyone pulling his or her share of the load.

DEVELOPING TEAM COMMUNICATION

The final aspect of developing team-building skills to be discussed in this chapter regards skill in developing team communication. The goal here is to develop open channels for all the communication necessary for successful completion of the team project. Perhaps the simplest way for a leader to develop an effective communication climate in the team is by setting an example in his or her own communication with them. There are five characteristics the leader can show that will have a powerful influence on the quality of communication among team members. These are (1) honesty, (2) openness, (3) constructiveness, (4) adultness, and (5) respect.

Being Honest

This means behaving with fairness and integrity, not trying to manipulate others or "play games" with them.

Being Open

This means being willing to let others know your true feelings, not trying to hide your reactions behind a poker face.

Being Constructive

This means you should be constructively caring and working at three growth areas: first, pursuing your own self-development; second, helping each individual team member grow; third, building teamwork. It also means discouraging destructive behaviors which arouse feelings of fear or defensiveness.

Being Adult

This means you should strive for equality, for an adult-to-adult, rather than parent-to-child relationship with team members. In other words, level with them, avoid talking down to them.

Being Respectful

Try to feel receptive to differing viewpoints and accepting of the rights of others to values that may differ from your own. Try to understand and respect the other individuals' needs, wants, aspirations, and self-fulfillment potentials. Try to avoid judging others or conveying a feeling of superiority in your interactions with them.

If you can follow these five steps in your role as team

leader, you will provide an example that your team members will begin to apply in dealing with you and with each other.

SUMMARY

In this chapter we discussed team-building skills as a set of learnable skills that can be acquired by virtually anyone. Opportunities for acquiring or improving team-building skill abound in daily life; one has merely to take advantage of them. The process of skill development follows a common pattern, regardless of the skill one may be trying to improve. When trying to improve interpersonal skills, the key lies in learning to read the feedback. This information is then used to adjust your perception and your overt behavior in order to improve your effectiveness. Good coaching can speed up skill development greatly.

Several component skills make up effective team building. Each of these may be thought of as a skill in its own right. These are skills in (1) self-understanding, (2) understanding individual team members, (3) understanding the team as a team, (4) planning team performance, and (5) developing team communication.

Self-understanding is a skill which can be learned. As with team-building skills in general, one way to begin is with self-assessments which you can then compare with assessments of how others see you. A useful starting point is to examine how you relate to others, then to examine your impact on others. The objective is to learn to see yourself as others see you. Another useful step in increasing self-understanding is to examine your team-building strengths and how you use or misuse them. Misuse is relying too heavily on one or two strengths rather then developing other strengths that are a part of effective team leadership skill. In addition to assessing your strengths, it is worth examining your weaknesses and how you have been coping with them. Because team leadership depends heavily on your ability to influence others, it is extremely useful to discover whether others agree with your self-assessment. They respond to your behavior as they see it, not as you see it.

Understanding your individual team members is a very important part of your role as a team leader. It too is a learnable skill. It depends on having a sincere interest in each member and trying to put yourself in the other person's shoes. A good place to start is by trying to understand the value systems and personal goals of the other individuals. What do they hope to get out of participation in the team activity? Another aspect is to develop some understanding of the motivational patterns of each team member. What basic need does each seem to be trying to satisfy? By careful observation the team leader can usually identify motivational patterns in team members. Esteem needs and belonging needs are at the core of many individual motivational patterns.

Since much of behavior is aimed at actualizing one's self-concept, it is very useful for the team leader to develop skill in understanding the self-concept of each team member. It is particularly important to be able to identify whether the member sees himself or herself as a winner or a loser with respect to the various team tasks. A related aspect of skill in understanding your individual team members lies in learning about the members' prior experiences with similar tasks and evaluating the skill and expertise that each member possesses. It is also very useful to know about past successes and past failures related to team performance and specific tasks that will need to be assigned. Finally, it is very important to understand how the various team members see you as a person and especially how they see your role as team leader. This will help identify possible obstacles to your effective leadership.

Understanding your team as a unit is a skill quite different from understanding them as individuals. It includes developing skill in assessing the experience and capability mix that are your basic resources as team leader. But it also includes developing awareness of existing interpersonal relationships between two or more team members. These may be either very positive or very negative and can pose problems. Because the essence of teamwork is interdependence, the leader must reinforce awareness of that fact if he or she hopes to achieve high team performance; team members must really believe that they need each other. Learning to evaluate the communication among group members is another important aspect of skill in understanding your team. Group communication reveals much about the cohesiveness and morale of the group at any point in time. The tuned-in leader can quickly take corrective action before minor problems become major ones.

Cohesiveness refers to the attraction group members have for one another. It is an indication of how much they like to be together. Cohesiveness is based on mutual need satisfaction, but does not guarantee high performance. Morale, on the other hand, refers to the confidence the team has in its ability to succeed. High-morale groups are often also highly cohesive. Because morale, either high or low, tends to function like a self-fulfilling prophecy, effective team leaders develop great sensitivity to the morale of their team. One of the best indicators of morale is the enthusiasm that team members show in their work. A final aspect of skill in understanding your team involves learning to assess their perception of your leadership role. The simplest way to avoid the consequences of mismatched expectations is through open, honest role negotiation. This way each person knows exactly what you expect and what to expect from you.

Successful team performance is rarely an accident. It is usually the result of very careful planning. Planning often provides a very effective means of getting team members really involved in the project from the very beginning. Planning usually begins with the establishment of very specific, quantifiable performance goals. The effective leader soon learns that fuzzy goals result in fuzzy performance. Once specific goals are set, the next step is detailed planning of the work required to achieve the goal, with attention to schedules and resources available. It also includes a breakdown of the overall effort into the various tasks that will have to be performed. At that point, individual team members and the leader are in a position to negotiate the assignment of specific tasks to the various team members. Because all the tasks that make up the team project are interdependent, minimum performance criteria must be established for each task. This reinforces expectations of high performance and more clearly defines them in everyone's mind. Finally, feedback on performance must be planned into the team effort. This is both to enable the team leader to track team progress and to permit team members to know how they are doing. Frequent feedback not only results in improved performance, but also has a favorable effect on team morale.

The final team leader skill discussed as necessary to effective team development is skill in developing team communication. The simplest way is for the leader to set the example in his or her own communication with team members. Five steps an effective leader can take are to be honest, to be open, to be constructive for growth, to be adult, and to be respectful in communications with team members. This mode of communication tends to be contagious.

ASSIGNMENTS

A. Team Skill Development Exercise

1. Form a group of about six class members (five or seven will do as well).

2. The group task is to plan a fund-raising activity to purchase books on business management for the school library.
3. Before working at the team task, have each member rate himself or herself on the Self-Rating of Team Leader Skills (Table 2).
4. Working together on the task, develop a team following the processes discussed in this chapter.
5. After the team has completed its plan and prepared a presentation for the class, have team members rate themselves and their teammates.
6. Each team member should then compare his or her own original rating (taken before the team exercise) with a self-rating made after the exercise. Were they the same? If not, how were self-perceptions changed?
7. Each team member should compare the second self-rating with the ratings given by teammates. Do the ratings agree? If not, how do self-perceptions differ from teammates' perceptions? What can account for the differences?

B. Coaching Exercise

1. Based on your Self-Rating of Team Leader Skills, pair off with a class member who rates himself or herself low in a skill area on which you rate yourself high.
2. Negotiate a coaching relationship to help strengthen performance in the area of weakness.
3. Plan the performance situations which will be followed by coaching sessions using the Coaching Checklist in Chapter Three.
4. Follow the plan and prepare a report on the experience.

C. Self-development Exercise

1. Based on your Self-Rating of Team Leader Skills, pair off with a class member who has considerable skill in an area in which you feel you are weak.

2. Negotiate a coaching relationship to help you improve your performance in the weak skill area.
3. Plan the performance situations which will be followed by coaching sessions.
4. Follow the plan and prepare a report on the experience.

REFERENCES

HARRIS, THOMAS A. *I'm OK—You're OK*. New York: Harper & Row, 1967.

JAMES, MURIEL, AND JONGEWARD, DOROTHY. *Born to Win: Transactional Analysis with Gestalt Experiments*. Menlo Park, Ca.: Addison-Wesley, 1971.

NIERENBERG, GERARD. *Fundamentals of Negotiating*. New York: Hawthorne Books, 1973.

SCHUTZ, WILLIAM C. *The Interpersonal Underworld*, reprint ed. Palo Alto, Ca.: Science and Behavior Books, 1966.

SCHUTZ, WILLIAM C. *Firo-B*. Palo Alto, Ca.: Consulting Psychologists Press, 1967. (Questionnaire forms, scoring keys, and Manual may be purchased from the publisher.)

SHOSTROM, EVERETT L. *Man the Manipulator*. New York: Bantam Books, 1967.

PANEL DISCUSSION

Ends: Chapter Four deals with the acquisition and development of team-building skills by the would-be manager. Suppose a young person suddenly realizes that to get ahead in this world he has to learn how to take a group of peers and build them into a team in order to get a job done. So the question is: If team leadership skills are the ones that he needs, how does he go about developing them, assuming that he hasn't already developed them. Of course, some people start this very early in life and kind of fall into it. But now here's a person who says, "If I'm going to succeed in business, I'm going to have to know how to do this." How do you suggest he go about it? Shirley, I thought I heard you earlier saying we can start right in the classroom, that there's some opportunity for developing these skills through opportunities for participation in organizing things in the classroom, participating in classroom discussion, things like that.

Covington: He can also get it through team activities in sports.

Chilton: Selecting his fellow participants on a committee, team tennis, or baseball is the beginning of management practice. Not enough emphasis is placed on these school-related decisions as a foundation for management techniques of the future leaders of business and government. The importance of working together at the things "we can do best" outside of sports plays an important role in the growth of each student. But we don't really *tell* them that . . . or even more important . . . *show* them.

Covington: I would guess that a high percentage of our high achievers were also high achievers of one kind or another during their school days. That's one of the things that I look at when I'm interviewing.

Page: You wouldn't say though that they were necessarily achieving what it was that the school wanted them to achieve.

Covington: Oh, no.

Chilton: You are right, Bob, it's what the achiever has discovered, but there are others who could do the same thing. They are the late bloomers who need encouragement. They may have selected what they want to achieve too.

Ends: Do you think nearly anyone could learn these skills if they wanted to, or is it only people who seem to be naturally dominant that fall into these roles? Do you think they set out deliberately to learn them?

Chilton: I don't think everyone can learn management skills. It depends too much on family, social, and educational background. I believe *management concepts* can be learned, but the ability to execute, build a team, and motivate—not necessarily. If someone does not want to manage, no matter what you try it won't be effective.

Covington: Well, if they're self-motivated, then I think there is a high probability that they can.

Chilton: Right, but I don't think everyone can.

Kruel: She said, "if they don't want to."

Page: Well, suppose they want to?

Chilton: Some people are highly motivated to *want* to manage but not highly motivated *to learn how* to manage. Something else I want to include in this discussion is the family environment as the first threshold for learning team-building skills. The family is where you learn cooperation and compassion. I don't want that confused with involvement in associates' lives. Empathy is one thing, but expression of real compassion for your associate, your family, the human race may be another. If you can get that ingredient, that concern, that thoughtfulness stirring around within a manager it is a tremendous base for motivation and understanding of their subordinates' talents and abilities. The ability of the team to work together influences their attitudes toward each other and that is what a manager can bring out and emphasize through his own understanding of each individual on the team. However, one thing we have to guard against is getting too much behavioral dominance involved in a team. It is necessary to have the sensitivity to recognize when behavioral activity is consuming the group as opposed to accomplishing the task which needs to be done. Everyone has a different level of behavioral absorption. No one individual responds to the same level of behavioral concerns as the next one, and motivation of some team members can be dissipated, a few requiring or demanding "overstroking."

Page: I want to throw another word in there and it's *process*, because I think what you're saying is, "When are we going to stop this processing, and get on with the job? When are we going to stop talking about *how* we're doing this and *how* we're relating to each other and get that task done?"

Chilton: By all means, it can lead to process stagnation or to overstroking part of the group and understroking the balance. Through all this exercise you suffer "objective dilution." You don't know where you're going because you haven't decided what tasks to perform. All you've done is spent a lot of time spinning your wheels.

Covington: I think one of the things that you mentioned, Shirley, that ought to be geared toward the young person is that of the family impact. You can use it both as a positive and a negative thing because of the family problems and the family successes that are true today in a strong family unit. Frequently you have a real team process there—with the parents in a leadership role, the children participating. There are numerous examples and you probably will be able to think of them in line with your own experience; where there is no leadership from the parents the children have to develop self-motivation.

Chilton: Quite often that self-motivation comes out stronger when you have parental conflict.

Covington: It can, if the individual has a strong enough character.

Farrell: Let's get some concrete examples of what we're talking about, particularly in those areas where you're talking about a theory that's rather conceptual.

Page: I can give an illustration of a failure, I think. I know a person who wants very much to learn team-building skills, so I feel the motivation is there. It's not that he's resisting doing that, but I think that in terms of the self-assessment we've got a problem because he's really not in touch with himself. He does not understand himself well enough to really begin to understand his individual team members. What he does mostly is project his own desires and needs, etc., on his team members, rather than sit back and try to figure out where they are, then figure out how to understand the team by virtue of molding together the strengths and propping up the weaknesses of others, and so on.

Kruel: I think what you're describing is the very strong manager who doesn't have flexibility and who probably has been in the role for quite a period of time.

Page: In this case, yes. He's probably had about a ten-year history in this direction and now he wants to be a team man.

Ends: Well, Shirley, since you usually have the last word, I wonder if you would summarize our discussion of developing team-building skills?

Chilton: I've been taking notes as we rambled along—do you mind if I read them? Or would the coherence destroy the continuity of the discussion? (laughter)

Ends: Let's risk it!

Chilton: Well, in order to understand how to go about developing team-building skills, it is important first to identify the skills that a team member or a team manager must possess or develop in order to organize an effective group. Starting with the assumption that a group has come together without the benefit of a preselection process on the part of the team manager, the manager should develop his approach in the following manner:

1. *Consider the environment as set by the task to be performed:* For example, long-range planning can be more abstract and conceptual than writing procedures for a particular function. In addition, the style of management of the organization should be considered in order to ensure success in acceptance of the task. Is management paternalistic? rigidly structured? decentralized? etc.

2. *Evaluate the abilities, talents, and shortcomings of team members and managers:* Perception of strengths and their proper utilization in assigning functions, as well as weaknesses and the methods employed to overcome them, are vital to avoid productivity gaps in team performance.

3. *Provide concise interpretation and dissemination of facts concerning the task to be performed:* The ability to communicate what needs to be done through clear verbal and written instructions and reports is vital for all team members.

4. *Establish empathetic concern:* The ability to predict and understand the reactions of others to various ideas and situations facilitates the flow of ideas and enhances innovation.

5. *Maintain flexible perceptions:* The understanding of other team members' problems stemming from experience or background "hang-ups" is important in delegating and sharing work and gaining the support of all team members. This perception reduces feelings of insecurity and stimulates cooperation, which in turn motivates toward excellence in performance.

6. *Generate enthusiasm, vitality, and energetic leadership through example:* The dynamics of motivation can accomplish great strides through a catalytic, "gung-ho" team member. The energetic (and well-

directed) team member can set the example of work performance throughout the entire task.

7. *Delegate functions:* Judgment in allocating duties and the ability to let the team perform these duties is necessary in the continuing success of the group. A certain amount of dominance can be exercised from time to time by the team leader; however, the tendency to oversupervise can destroy motivation and the dynamics of accomplishment.

8. *Avoid overemphasis on interpersonal concerns:* Although group interfacing and cooperation is a key factor in the success of a team, excessive emphasis on personal reactions, feelings, etc., can lead to process stagnation. Such "overstroking" can dilute the effectiveness of the team.

9. *Listen:* Most of the skills listed above cannot be developed without receptive and analytical listening. Many people listen; few hear, and fewer hear and perceive. Of all the skills necessary for effective team development, listening is probably the most important and the most difficult to learn.

10. *Offer positive evaluation:* The team's ability to critically evaluate the job they have done is based upon the atmosphere in which feedback is established. An open, frank discussion of the task and the team will encourage improvement and bind the team together to achieve improvement. The ability of all team members to question positively will build a better format for the next task.

The young person entering business can start his very first day on the job using all of the above in the performance of his job and relationships with associates and supervisors. By evaluating the management style and corporate organizational image, he will be able to select a compatible approach which can simultaneously satisfy his own goals and objectives.

In understanding his own strengths and weaknesses with

an emphathetic awareness of the same traits in others, he will become a desirable co-worker and a participant of value.

Through his enthusiastic and energetic dedication to his job he can motivate associates and assume leadership among his peers.

By developing listening and hearing skills and critical evaluation techniques he will become an important arm of management by providing input for constructive solutions to problems which may otherwise go unrecognized.

By doing so, he will have automatically assumed a leadership role which hopefully management will acknowledge by welcoming him as a member of management.

Ends: Thank you, Shirley!

Chilton: You got in the last word that time!

five

The Team-building Process

OBJECTIVES

After reading Chapter Five you should be able to:

1. Discuss the overall process of team development.
2. List the steps a team leader must lead a group through in order to build it into a team.
3. Describe the importance of the team meeting in the team-building process.
4. Outline the activities carried on in team meetings and their effects on the success of the team-building effort.
5. Discuss the concept of Organization Development.

INTRODUCTION

The actual process of developing a group of people into a team worthy of the name will vary considerably from situation to situation. There is no magic formula that one can apply to all situations and automatically produce a high-performing team. Trying to build a team out of a group of enthusiastic volunteers who are meeting for the first time to put on a fund-raising rummage sale for the benefit of the church Christmas Basket fund is one thing. Trying to build a team out of a group of people who have worked together in the same office for some time, who have low morale, who are not very productive, and who have developed some strong positive as well as negative attitudes toward one another is quite a different thing. The chief differences lie in the amount of diagnostic work that must be done, the amount of effort that must go into resolving interpersonal conflicts of long standing, and the amount of time that must be spent in developing enthusiasm for the task at hand. It is nearly always easier to form and develop a new team than to build one from a group of people who have worked together for some length of time but have never found much satisfaction in their interaction. With a new team, the team leader can devote most of his or her effort to developing the team. With a group of people who have spent much time together on the job but have never functioned as a team, the leader will usually have to expend a great deal of effort undoing the mistakes of the past, healing old wounds, resolving old conflicts, and rectifying other such problems that might interfere with the development of a productive team until they have been effectively dealt with. However, in spite of the variations in details from situation to situation, there are certain common elements in the team-building process that occur, or should occur, in most situations. Since the variety of situations where team building is appropriate is limitless, we will examine only the common elements.

The process of team development is easier to understand if we consider it first in terms of how a manager or team leader might approach a team-development task, and the phases through which the leader takes the group to turn them into a team. Then we will examine the process in terms of the types of activities that must be performed on a continuous basis throughout the various phases in the life of the team. Finally we will briefly review the concept of organization development.

THE PHASES OF TEAM DEVELOPMENT

From the team leader's viewpoint, the process of team building may be divided into four phases: (1) undertaking initial analysis and preliminary diagnosis; (2) setting team goals and objectives; (3) planning the work; and (4) doing the work. It should be understood that there is usually some overlap among the phases.

Initial Analysis and Preliminary Diagnosis

When faced with the task of team building, the first thing the would-be team leader usually does is analyze the situation. In his or her own mind the team leader tries to answer such questions as these: What do I hope the team will be able to accomplish? How much time do we have to get the job done? What kind of people do I have as team members? What obstacles will I have to overcome? What is the best way to go about achieving our goals? Or, if the leader is trying to develop teamwork in an existing group, the initial analysis may begin with the question "What should we be doing better?" This may then be followed by a preliminary diagnosis which begins with the question "What is keeping us from performing more effectively?" (These, of course, are questions managers should be asking themselves rather frequently in any case.) The initial analysis and preliminary diagnosis is an important step in the team-building process even though the team leader may later wish to get the whole team involved in the diagnosis. It helps the leader understand the challenge the group is facing and helps him or her decide on the best way to tackle the team-building job. The leader must guard against "falling in love" with the diagnosis. Experience has shown that as often as not the initial diagnosis by any but the most experienced consultant or team leader is incomplete or misses the mark by a wide margin. Nevertheless, a tentative diagnosis, even if wrong, can still serve a useful purpose. It can be presented to the team as a starting point for a team discussion leading to a more accurate diagnosis on a group basis. The advantage of getting the entire team involved in diagnosing their difficulties is that it gets *everyone* thinking about how team performance can be improved.

Setting Team Goals and Objectives

Usually the team leader will have some pretty clear team performance goals and objectives in mind before meeting with the team for a goal-setting discussion. There are several reasons for this. First, the leader/manager is expected to know what the larger organization, of which the team is but a part, expects in the way of performance. If the leader has been chosen by the boss to form and lead a team to do a specific job, then he or she usually has been told what the minimum performance must be; for example, "Reduce delay in billing accounts receivable to no more than two days by the end of the quarter." When the team leader is given such a specific target, discussion with team members does not involve goal setting in the usual sense. Instead it involves communicating what is expected. Discussion may then revolve around whether the team members think they can achieve the goal. If the goal is a very demanding one, or if the team members have little confidence in themselves, or if morale is low, the discussion may generate more heat than light. The wise leader will allow the group to express their feelings of outrage, or of being put upon, or any other negative, resentful or hostile feelings they may have. This helps "bleed off" feelings of anger and frustration carried over from other experiences that actually have nothing to do with the new task at hand. If the leader can accept the expression of these negative feelings for what they are without getting defensive, the group will eventually wind down and be ready to address the problems at hand.

When the team turns to a discussion of the goal, whether

it is one handed down from above or whether the group has the option of setting its own goal, the team leader has two major concerns. The first concern is to make sure the team members will actually commit themselves to achieve the team goal. This means that most of the team members see the goal as not only achievable but also as desirable. And most important, they must be ready to work to achieve it. As mentioned in Chapter Four, if team members feel they have had a part in setting or accepting the goal, they are much more likely to make the commitment. It becomes *their* goal—not the leader's or the organization's—their very own. This is a very vital step in the team-building process.

The second major concern of the leader during goal-accepting or goal-setting discussions involves the team members as individuals. The leader's concern is to help each individual express the personal goals and objectives he or she would like to achieve as a member of the team. The purpose of this is to discover what each team member hopes to get out of the team experience. Unless the individual team member clearly sees "what's in it for me", commitment to the team goal may soon fade. An open discussion of what everyone hopes to get out of the effort can go a long way toward creating a climate of openness, honesty, and trust.

Planning the Work

The team leader should have at least the rough outlines of a plan in mind. Team members usually expect the leader to provide at least the first cut at how to proceed. Again, the leader will try to secure commitment to the details of the plan by encouraging team members to participate in the planning. One of the leader's concerns during the action-planning discussion is to arrive at a plan that integrates individual and team goals as much as possible. If one of the members wants the opportunity to develop a new skill such as selling, rather than being limited to, say, the usual record-keeping role, the leader and the group should aid that development if it does not jeopardize the success of the team endeavor. The planning process should allow for such instances of group negotiation of individual roles. Roles should be negotiated openly among team members if the nature of the task permits it. When open role negotiations are part of the planning process, the concerns of the leader are twofold: (1) to make sure they are carried out with fairness to all members, and (2) to make sure that the role assignments being negotiated do not seriously reduce the chance of team success. The team leader has one additional major concern during the group planning process. This concern is to incorporate the achievement pattern into the emerging detailed plan, with special attention to the need for performance feedback to each member and to the team as a whole.

Doing the Work

Once the work of the team has actually begun, the team-building process really moves into high gear. The team leader performs major functions aimed at developing people into a high-performing team. First he or she must maintain high performance standards for the team and for the individual team members. The leader's conviction that the team and each of the members are capable of a high level of performance helps to reinforce the resolve of the team members. The leader's belief in the team and his or her enthusiasm for the job to be done have a very positive effect on morale, providing the leader also performs other necessary functions well.

The second major function of the team leader during this phase is to make sure that each team member gets the support, cooperation, direction, supervision, and coaching that he or she needs to fulfill an assigned role on the team. This does not mean that the leader does all these things; the job is to make sure they are available to the member when needed.

The third major function of the team leader in this phase is to assure that each member receives more or less continuous feedback on performance. The leader must also provide feedback to the team as a whole on team performance. Remember, people cannot improve their performance unless they know how well they are doing. Team "howgozit" meetings are very useful devices which permit all team members to air their gripes and discuss the difficulties they may be having in fulfilling their respective team roles. Such meetings also help the team leader identify who needs extra individual coaching in order to perform assigned tasks adequately. They also provide an opportunity to give recognition for good performance and for improvement shown in performance.

The fourth major function of the leader in the work phase is the evaluation of overall group performance. The leader alone has the overview of the entire team effort. He or she must evaluate total team performance against schedule, plan, use of resources, and performance standards. In other words, the leader has the responsibility for seeing to it that the entire operation is on target, and if it is not, that person must decide what to do about it.

THE CONTINUOUS PROCESSES

While any team must go through the various phases of team development in some fashion, if the leader wants to ensure that the team will be cohesive, will develop high morale, and will be highly successful, he or she must devote considerable effort to the improvement of two related but distinct processes. These are the group interaction process and the growth process of the individual team members. We will discuss only the group interaction process first, because if it is handled well it can help enormously to support and stimulate the performance growth process of the individual team members. It should be noted that while the team leader may be mostly concerned with the growth in performance of individual team members, performance growth in a supportive team setting invariably results in personal growth for the team members as well.

Improving the Group Interaction Process

The team leader's concern with the quality of the group interaction process—how the members interact in doing the work of the team—is a never-ending one. The leader's concern begins with the formation of the team and ends only when the team is disbanded. Throughout all phases of team development the leader must work steadily to improve the group interaction process. As a general rule, team success depends more on the quality of the group interaction process than on any other single variable.

The Team Meeting

The primary vehicle used by the team leader to develop and improve the group interaction process is the team meeting. The leader begins to establish influence on group-member interaction at the very first team meeting and never relaxes the effort during the life of the team. It makes little difference what phase of development the group may be in, whether diagnosing, goal setting, planning, or doing the work. However, because the group interaction process influences group task performance, and vice versa, the leader must be concerned with making the team meetings productive from a task viewpoint as well as from a process viewpoint. In a typical team meeting both task and process considerations are involved. As a consequence, the team leader as well as some of the group members may be shifting back and forth between task and process inputs to the ongoing discussion. Some of these inputs will have the effect of helping the group make progress toward the goal of the meeting, others will have the effect of strengthening group cohesiveness and solidarity. On the other hand, some inputs will have the effect of interfering with group progress toward its goal or impairing the growth of group cohesiveness and solidarity. The leader's task, of course, is to stimulate the group members to make mostly beneficial inputs and to minimize detrimental inputs. He or she does this by developing a supportive and productive climate in the team meetings. The more successful the leader is at creating and maintaining such a climate, the faster the team can grow in capability. The reason for this is that in a supportive climate, team members' energies can be devoted to constructive effort rather than wasted on defensiveness or destructive attacks on others in the group. Because the leader wants to get the team members involved as much as possible, he or she sets the example for effective participation and encourages others to gradually assume responsibility for the same kind of behavior. As the team members become more involved, more responsible, and more effective in providing the necessary inputs or services to the team-building effort, the leader must still provide whatever services the members may not have provided in a specific meeting. Let us look briefly at these services or contributions to the improvement of task performance and team interaction.

Task-oriented Services or Contributions

These activities may be performed by the team leader or by any team member. They are services to the group because they help the group to make progress toward the goal of the group meeting, whether it be to diagnose a problem, set goals, or plan the activity.

Energizing This activity consists of suggesting new ideas, proposing solutions to problems, offering new definitions of the problems, proposing a new approach to a problem, or coming up with a new way of organizing the data the group may be working with. This kind of activity provides the spark for group discussion.

Searching This activity consists of such things as asking for clarification of suggestions that have been made and requesting additional information or facts. This kind of activity helps the person making the suggestion realize that the suggestion has not been fully understood and gives that person an opportunity to explain it more clearly. It also helps to make sure that all team members have a better understanding of the proposal being discussed.

Polling This activity involves looking for an expression of feeling about something from the whole group. As the term *polling* implies, it is an attempt to find out where the group stands with regard to a suggestion, an idea, or even to the group values. This kind of activity is a service to the group because it helps the group decide whether there is enough support from the members to continue considering some proposal or suggestion or to drop it. It is also useful in helping a group discover whether it has already made a decision and need spend no more time discussing the pros and cons.

Evaluating This activity consists of stating an opinion or belief concerning a suggestion or proposal—particularly concerning its value with respect to helping the group achieve its goals, not whether the suggestion or proposal is factually or technically sound. This sort of activity can be of service to the group because it helps keep the discussion on track. It helps keep the group from wasting time considering things that may be interesting to some members, but which do not help the group progress toward its goals.

Summarizing This activity consists of pulling together related suggestions after the group has discussed them. This activity is a service to the group because it helps tie all the pertinent points together in a neat, easy-to-understand package. This enables each team member to check his or her own understanding of what took place and what was agreed on in the discussion up to that point. If everyone agrees with the summary, then the group knows it is safe to proceed to the next topic.

Group Process Services or Contributions

These activities may also be performed either by the leader or by any team member. In the early stages of team development, the leader often has to provide the lion's share of these services until the team members begin to get the hang of it. These activities are services to the group because they help pull the group together, strengthen group solidarity, and maintain integrity of the group once team spirit has begun to develop.

Encouraging This type of activity includes being friendly, warm, and responsive to other group members and their ideas. It also consists of expressing agreement with and acceptance of the various contributions of others when sincerely meant. While many members may *feel* friendly and accepting of the other team members, such feelings have little effect on the group interaction process unless they are expressed. Such expressions, when genuinely meant, are a service to the group because they help to create a supportive team climate.

Including The essence of this type of activity is trying to make it possible for another member to make a contribution to the group. This may take the form of statements such as,

"We haven't heard anything from Karen yet" or "Perhaps we should limit everyone to five minutes to present a position on the proposal so that everyone has a chance to be heard." This sort of activity is a service to the group because it helps to draw the shy or more quiet members into the discussion, and helps prevent the more talkative members from dominating the discussion.

Standardizing This kind of activity involves expressing standards for the group to use in choosing discussion topics, or in selecting procedures to follow, or in arriving at decisions. It also reminds the group to avoid decisions that conflict with group standards. Such activities are a service to the group because they help the group to develop ground rules for carrying on discussions and define and reinforce group rules, procedures, and values.

Ventilating This type of activity amounts to summarizing the group consensus or describing the *reactions* of the group to ideas or solutions. Examples are statements such as, "It seems that none of us really likes that approach" or "I get the feeling that everyone feels very good about our progress so far." Such statements are a service to the group because they bring out into the open what everyone seems to be feeling, and also because they provide an opportunity for those who do not agree to make their feelings known.

Group Task and Group Process Services

These activities by their very nature tend to not only help the group progress toward the discussion-task goal, but also help to improve the group interaction process at the same time. While they therefore do double duty, they are also activities that require a little more skill to carry out effectively. In the early stages of team development, the leader should be prepared to provide most of these services.

Evaluating Constructive evaluating activity consists of comparing group decisions or accomplishments with group standards, or measuring accomplishments against goals. To be constructive, evaluating should be phrased in such a way that it does not "point fingers" or put others on the defensive. An example of constructive evaluation might be, "We seem to have arrived at a decision, but I feel it falls short of the standards we agreed on. Does anyone else see it that way?" Such statements are a service to the group because they not only help the group keep on track in getting its job done, but also help improve the group process by reinforcing concern for group standards and the idea that all group members are equally responsible for group decisions.

Diagnosing This activity is mainly trying to determine the sources of difficulties the group is having in making progress, trying to ascertain appropriate steps to take next, or trying to identify the main blocks to progress. An example of a diagnosing statement might be, "I think the reason we are having so much trouble in agreeing on a plan is that we really haven't agreed on what we want to accomplish." Activity of this kind provides a service to the group because such statements not only help the group identify roadblocks to progress toward the goal, but also help the group to examine the interaction processes that may have created the block in the first place.

Testing This type of activity consists of tentatively asking for group opinions in order to find out whether the group is nearing consensus on a decision, or sending up trial balloons to test group opinions. An example of such a statement might be, "Have we discussed this enough so we are ready to make a decision?" or "I think Jane would be the ideal person to handle that task, does everyone agree?" Statements of this type are a service to the group because they help save group time that might otherwise be spent discussing something long after agreement had been reached but not communicated openly. It helps the group interaction process because it invites each member to verbalize an opinion with respect to the question without forcing agreement if it doesn't really exist.

Mediating Activity under this label includes harmonizing or reconciling differences in points of view between several group members or coming up with compromise solutions to problems in a way that will be acceptable to the persons in disagreement. An example might be a statement such as, "You and Joe are not really as far apart as you may think. If you could juggle your schedule to get him a rough draft by next Wendesday, he could use that to go ahead with his work and incorporate any changes resulting from your final report when you are satisfied that it is ready for release. Would that work for both of you?" Again, such statements help keep the work moving and improve the group process by resolving conflicts that can lead to hostility and resentment, thus destroying group effectiveness. Care must be taken when mediating that viewpoints are actually reconciled and the compromises actually accepted by those involved. If agreement is forced, group disunity is in the making.

Conciliating This kind of activity—joking, or pouring oil on troubled waters—serves to drain off negative feeling. It also includes statement aimed at putting a tense situation into a wider context. Humorous quips, if well timed, can often do much to relieve growing tension and conflict between members. Conflict between a male and a female team member, for example, might be relieved by some such comment as, "You two act like you're married." Or putting a tense situation into broader context might take the form of, "If you're going to get so up-tight about this, what are you going to do when we get into the really important problems?" Since conflict and tension usually interfere with group progress, conciliating helps the group keep moving. It also helps improve the interaction process because it drains off tension before it can build to unmanageable proportions. It also demonstrates that the group is able to cope with tensions without permanent damage or ejection of members. It helps to create a supportive climate.

Detrimental Behavior

From time to time, more often perhaps than anyone likes to admit, people behave in ways that do not help the group, but instead slow down or delay the process and sometimes actually harm the group, its members, or the work it is trying to do. Some of the more common types of such detrimental activities are described below.

Attacking Working for status by criticizing or blaming others, showing hostility against the group or some individual, or deflating the ego or status of others.

Blocking Interfering with the progress of the group by going off on a tangent, citing personal experiences unrelated to the problem, arguing too much on a point, or rejecting ideas without consideration.

Competing Openly or subtly engaging in competition with others to produce the best idea, talk the most, and play the most roles.

Pleading Introducing or supporting suggestions related to one's own pet concerns, philosophies, or biases.

Clowning Joking, mimicking, and disrupting work of the group.

Handclasping Seeking to establish a relationship with one other participant to ease tension, or carrying on a dialogue with that person at the expense of group time.

Striving Attempting to call attention to oneself by loud or excessive talking, extreme ideas, or unusual behavior.

Isolating Acting indifferent or passive, resorting to excessive formality, daydreaming, doodling, whispering to others, wandering from the subject.

Honeymooning Trying to make it appear that everyone in the group loves everyone else in order to avoid a personally threatening situation.

In using these classifications we must guard against the tendency to blame the person (whether self or others) who acts in such a way. It is more useful to regard such behavior as an indication that all may not be well with the group's ability to satisfy individual needs through group-centered activity.

Between Team Meetings

The team-building efforts of the leader are not confined to the team meetings of course. The leader must take advantage of every opportunity to improve the group interaction process and to reinforce commitment to group goals. He or she must keep a watchful eye open for indications of frustration, flagging spirits, or signs of interpersonal conflict among team members. Such conditions, if not dealt with as soon as they are noticeable, can lead to rapid deterioration of the team spirit the leader has worked so hard to develop.

At this point most readers will agree that there is much more to being an effective team builder and team leader than meets the eye. The important point to keep in mind is that building and leading a team is not a single skill, but rather a complex of component skills that taken together are often loosely referred to as leadership skill. To help you remember some of the main points you must attend to when you are trying to build a high-performing team, Table 5-1 may be of use.

AFTER TEAM BUILDING?

Because the world is changing at an incredibly rapid rate, many approaches to management and organization that were

Table 5-1. Team Builder's Checklist

_____ 1. Does each team member, including myself, have a crystal clear understanding of the agreed goals of the team?

_____ 2. Is every team member, including myself, sufficiently committed to the team goals to devote the necessary effort to achieve them?

_____ 3. Does every team member, including myself, clearly understand his or her assigned role on the team and the importance of that role to team success?

_____ 4. Is every team member, including myself, committed to fulfilling his or her assigned role to the best of his or her ability?

_____ 5. Does every team member, including myself, clearly understand the plan for reaching team goals and, especially, does every team member understand precisely the part of the planned activity he or her is responsible for?

_____ 6. Does every team member, including myself, understand and accept the performance standards for individual activity and the total team activity necessary for the team to achieve its goals?

_____ 7. Am I providing frequent, timely, and useful feedback on each team member's performance, and to the team as a whole on team performances?

_____ 8. Am I providing the coaching and supervision necessary to help each team member and the group as a whole reach the required performance standards?

_____ 9. Am I providing the initiative, the enthusiasm, the sense of purpose, and an example of appropriate behavior and attitudes that team members expect of their leader?

_____10. Am I creating and maintaining a supportive group climate, and am I constructively controlling the group process?

quite satisfactory in the past are no longer effective. More and more people in business and government are searching for ways to make their organizations more effective. From this continuing search, a discipline known as *Organization Development* (OD) has evolved. The field of OD is still emerging, but its general outlines are presented here to acquaint you with the basic concept. This is not only because OD applies the ideas and methods discussed in previous chapters, but also because an increasing number of organizations are turning to OD to help improve their effectiveness. While many books and articles have been written on OD, in this chapter we will cover only two major aspects of it. These are (1) the OD concept, and (2) the team as the fundamental unit of change in OD.

The OD Concept

First of all, OD is a process. It is the process of discovering and applying more meaningful and more effective ways to get work done. The general assumption underlying OD is that the effectiveness of an organization depends largely on the ability of the organization to freely draw on the skills and the creativity of its human resources to cope with the problems generated by the ever-changing internal and external environment. Faced with continual change and the problems it creates, the manager's dilemma is how to (1) mobilize the energy and talent of the work force to achieve the organization's performance objectives, and (2) create at the same time an organization with a climate that stimulates commitment, involvement, and high performance from all. The OD process is designed to help the manager solve this dilemma. As currently practiced, OD has four basic characteristics which help distinguish it from other approaches to improving organizations.

OD Is a Planned Change Effort

An OD program is seldom initiated when things are going very well for an organization. Just as few happy, productive people seek personal psychotherapy, few organizations embark on OD programs unless someone, usually someone at the top, feels the organization is hurting. Typically the OD program begins when a key executive calls in an OD consultant for help in dealing with specific organizational problems such as low productivity or poor product quality. The consultant views these problems as the *result* of organizational ineffectiveness. In other words, he or she views them as symptoms rather than causes. This viewpoint in turn leads to a systematic diagnosis of the organization which usually begins with a clarification and restatement of the goals of the organization. Without a pretty clear idea of what an organization is trying to accomplish, it is virtually impossible to develop a plan. Lack of clear, meaningful goals or objectives is often at the root of organizational difficulties. Once the goals are clarified, the diagnostic process begins in earnest. Ideally, it eventually involves everyone in the organization who may have something to contribute. Once the diagnosis is made, a strategic plan for improvement is developed. Again, ideally planning will eventually involve everyone who will be affected by the planned change. Once the plan is agreed on, organizational resources are mobilized to carry out the effort. All this does not happen at the same time. OD tends to be a slow process in large organizations which starts at the top and gradually works down through the organization, department by department and level by level.

OD Increases the Effectiveness of the Organization

Effectiveness in achieving both short-term and long-term goals in a changing environment depends a great deal on how well the organization is geared to adapting to and coping with changes in the environment. Thus the aim of OD is to some-how improve the capacity of the organization to adapt and to cope. This often involves changes in the formal organizational structure, usually involves changes in internal procedures, and always involves changes in the attitudes, performance, and interpersonal interactions of the people in the organization.

OD Works through Planned Interventions in Processes and Tasks

In the diagnostic phase, both process and task have been examined and discussed in some detail by members of the organization. Those processes and tasks that were identified as sources of organizational ineffectiveness become targets for planned change. For example, if the intergroup process between the Sales Department and the Production Depart-ment involves hostility and distrust, that has the net effect of losing customers and increasing costs, and intervention in this ongoing process would be part of the OD planned change. Or, if the way assembly tasks were broken down to individual work stations in the factory resulted in worker boredom and a costly high turnover rate among assembly employees, an in-tervention into the task design would be included in the OD planned change. Because OD deals with the organization as a total system, virtually any aspect of organizational function-ing may become the target of planned intervention.

OD Deals Primarily with Groups

One of the assumptions of OD is that groups or teams, not individuals, are the basic building blocks of organizations. It is the group or team that changes under the OD concept.

The Team as the Unit of Change

While, as we have discussed in previous chapters, team performance depends on how well the individual members perform their assigned roles, OD is not primarily concerned with individuals as such. Team performance, not individual performance, is the concern of OD. But if team performance does not change unless individual team members change, then who, in an OD effort, is responsible for the necessary individual change and growth? The answer should be obvious: the team leader. Thus, in the final analysis, the success of OD is in large measure dependent on the team-building skills of the individual team leaders in the organization. When OD efforts fail, the failure is most often due to inadequate team-building skills on the parts of various team leaders in the organization.

Since the fundamental unit of change in OD is the team, perhaps it can be readily seen that what it changes is the organization. When one builds a team one also is building the organization. When the team changes, the nature of the organization changes. Thus the value and power of team leadership skills can hardly be overestimated.

A FINAL WORD

In this brief volume, we have tried to provide you with an awareness of what organizations are all about, a description of the nature of a manager's job, a presentation of key concepts in team building, some pointers on how to go about developing team-building skills, some examples of how these skills are applied, and a brief discussion of organization development as a new and growing management technology. That is a very large order in so short a text. We hope that we have left you with the clear realization that team-building and team-leadership skills can be yours if you are but willing to seek out the limitless opportunities to develop them. Your decision to deliberately acquire and improve these skills can well be one of the most important decisions of your career. Team-building skill will always be in great demand and short supply. Taking advantage of that ideal market is up to you: It is your choice.

SUMMARY

This chapter provides an overview of the team-building process and how a manager might approach the task of turning a group of people into a high-performing team. From the leader's viewpoint, the process of team development consists of four overlapping phases.

The first phase consists of *initial analysis and preliminary diagnosis*. In this phase, the leader is trying to size up the task, the human resources available, and what problems must be faced. If the leader is forming a new team, he or she will perform most of the work in this phase. If dealing with an existing group, the leader may solicit the help of team members to help with this activity, especially with the diagnostic effort.

The second phase of team building concerns *setting team goals and objectives*. While the leader is expected to have some pretty clear goals and objectives in mind if he or she wants a high-performing team, it is vital that the team members be involved as much as possible in the goal-setting activity. The purpose of this involvement is to secure the commitment of group members to the team goals. This is much more likely to occur if they have had a hand in setting them. Another reason to get group members involved in this phase is that it increases the probability that each member will clearly understand what the team is trying to accomplish. Finally, it gets group members to start thinking about what role they may wish to take in the team effort.

The third phase of team building is *planning the work* to be done. Again the leader is expected to have at least a rough, preliminary plan as a starting point for the group discussion. As with goal setting, the more the group members become involved in the planning process, the more likely they are to become committed to making it work. Joint planning with all team members participating also permits each team member to get a clear idea of what his or her role will be in the team effort, what the organization expects, what to expect from others, and what is in it for team members personally. Joint planning provides an opportunity for open negotiation of an individual role by each team member in concert with all other team members. This has the additional benefit of clarifying each person's perception of his or her own special role and gives each an opportunity to make sure that that role is acceptable.

Doing the work constitutes the fourth phase of team building. This is the phase during which the team-building process moves into high gear, if the first three phases have been handled well. The team leader spends much of his time during this phase performing four major functions: (1) The team leader maintains high performance standards for the team as a whole and for the individual members. (2) He or she makes sure that each team member gets all the help needed to fulfill a role on the team. (3) The leader makes sure that each team member receives frequent feedback on individual performance and provides the team with feedback on performance of the team as a whole. The use of "howgozit" meetings not only provides for open, team-oriented feedback, but also enables the leader to keep a finger on the pulse of the developing group process. (4) The leader evaluates overall group performance against schedule, plan, resource use, and quality standards. If performance in any of these areas is off target, the leader must take some kind of action.

While the four phases of team building consist of over-lapping but essentially different kinds of activities from the team leader's viewpoint, there is yet another kind of process that must concern her or him continuously. This is the quality of the group interaction process. Using the team meeting as the primary vehicle, the leader helps the group to become more effective in accomplishing the task at hand and more effective in working together as human beings. Thus, throughout all phases of team building, the leader is concerned with both the effectiveness of the team in doing its work and the quality of the group interaction process—how the team members interact with one another as people. This dual concern is based upon the fact that group task performance and the group interaction process are highly interdependent in high-performing teams.

To help the group make progress toward its task goals, specific services must be performed by the leader or some group member in the team meetings. These services include energizing, searching, polling, evaluating, and summarizing. Services that improve the group interaction process include encouraging, including, standardizing, and ventilating. Some services, while more difficult to provide, improve both task performance and the interaction process at the same time. These are evaluating, diagnosing, testing, mediating, and conciliating. Some behaviors have a detrimental effect on the group interaction process and therefore on task performance as well. These are attacking, blocking, competing, pleading, clowning, handclasping, striving, isolating, and honeymooning.

Organization Development is a planned change effort. Its purpose is to increase the effectiveness of the organization in achieving its goals. It works through planned interventions in both process and task and is concerned primarily with groups or teams. It focuses on the team, rather than the individual, as the fundamental unit of change. Its success is therefore heavily dependent on the managers' team-building skills.

ASSIGNMENTS

A. Learning to Recognize Task-oriented Contributions

1. Organize the class into groups of no more than six to eight students each, making sure there are an even number of groups.
2. Pair off the groups, designating one of the two groups as *observers* and the other as the *task discussion group.*
3. Each task discussion group selects a discussion topic, such as planning a school dance, organizing a fund-raising drive, operating a small part-time business, or something similar.
4. The observers observe the discussion group so that there is one observer for each discussant.
5. The discussion group arranges itself in a small circle and begins the discussion.
6. The observer group arranges its members in a circle surrounding the discussion group circle.
7. Using the list of task-oriented contributions, observers should note what kinds of task-oriented contributions the person they are observing makes in the first fifteen minutes of the discussion and how often the person makes contributions.
8. At the end of fifteen minutes, call time out and have each observer give feedback on what he or she observed to the person being observed.

B. Learning to Recognize Group Process Contributions

1. Repeat Exercise A, except this time use the list of group process contributions.

REFERENCES

BECKHARD, RICHARD. *Organization Development: Strategies and Models.* Reading, Mass.: Addison-Wesley, 1969.

MARGULIES, NEWTON, AND RAIA, ANTHONY P. *Organizational Development: Values, Process, and Technology.* New York: McGraw-Hill, 1972.

SCHEIN, EDGAR H. *Process Consultation: Its Role in Organizational Development.* Reading, Mass.: Addison-Wesley, 1969.

BRADFORD, L. P. (ed.). *Group Development.* Washington, D.C.: National Training Laboratories, 1961.

CRIBBEN, J. J. *Effective Managerial Leadership.* New York: American Management Association, 1972.

PANEL DISCUSSION

Page: I wonder if we might get Walt's thoughts on the team-building process and, as we look at it, let's see what is necessary and sufficient in a team-building process; see whether we can identify skills that people must have in order to accomplish that process.

Kruel: I have a couple of examples. The ideal situation is that if you have people involved in the planning and they do contribute something to plan, you do have their contribution. It's an involvement—they become associated with it because it's partially theirs. Then when the work is to be done, it becomes easier because they see the reasons, the methods, the mechanics of doing it. Because they are involved they are committed to it and the reason for doing things becomes a lot clearer. I suspect what they have helped plan gets a lot more attention than something someone else told them to do.

When it comes to reviewing progress, I think the same thing is true. With that original commitment, the barrier to review is not quite as severe. The critique is more palatable—it doesn't destroy it totally. If you have someone report on their progress it's one thing, but if *you* report on that progress it is something else. That's what I am saying—that reviewing really should be more participative initially. I found the best exposure and solutions to problems come when people involved in doing the work expose the problem first, and then solutions are more readily acceptable. Well, I guess I keep stressing commitment in involvement.

Page: The young worker who is hoping to move into supervision, hoping to learn management, learns first about the "action steps" he is doing on the job. And then perhaps his supervisor explains to him "that's because we've got this goal out there, Charlie, . . ." So he starts at the bottom with his work, the action steps, and then the goal that is related to them. Then he might think about there being something else. There must be a strategy that these goals fall within, and then there must be some very broad objectives, and then all of that must relate somehow, in somebody's mind, to what we call "situation descriptions" of the future, what we think that future will be.

Chilton: I think that's what I wanted to say when I said you've got to evaluate the environment you're in. If it isn't what you want it to be, then you set a goal; you change your objectives, goals, and strategies if you want to make some change.

Page: Yes, I think the basis for developing a goal is basically a situation description of what you want the future to be. It aims you at a selection of a goal. You can change that any time the information base changes, or any time you find a goal that cannot be reached.

Covington: Well, I think in the "review process" involving employees with the department head, you can lessen the possibility of their feeling threatened if you use this approach: "Should we continue this program that you are involved in? Do we need to change its direction?" This helps them contribute to the goal-setting process and at the same time you get an evaluation of their own performance, and they indicate to you what they can do to be more effective. In the County we use what is called a Budget Target in developing our budget each year. It really isn't anything innovative, but it's surprising how many county, state, federal, or city governments do not do this because they have what they see as an unlimited source of funds through taxes. We're trying to overcome this by telling the department heads who have to prepare the initial budget request, "You've got a target to shoot for; you give me a budget that's within that target." It really helps them think and yet it doesn't put them into a threatening situation.

Chilton: That is just the way, in my opinion, that the reviewing process should be handled. When you involve them, that motivates them to be creative and innovative when their input is valued.

Page: Dave, you undoubtedly are running into situations where indeed you have people without very good team-building skills and you want to give them those skills and then you want them to practice those skills. Can you share with us any experiences you've had or are anticipating?

Farrell: First of all, we've identified those areas where we need special effort to get the team going. In terms of developing the person who is going to be leading the team, they have got to have a good sense of where they're coming from—understand themselves first—so that they can understand what they're projecting into the situation and so they can be more objective. Specifically, in how it relates to them and how they build the team, if people are going to be given more authority and responsibility for participating in setting goals or setting action items and generally controlling their own job, you've got to have the tools to do that. One of the basic tools is the knowledge that is necessary. I think Walt said that in other ways a couple of times. If this is going to be a real expansion of what they're doing, their normal exposure in the past may not have given them the data, the information, the techniques, and so forth. It's a long process and I think it has to be used as an investment if they did it over a period of many years, but not over a short term. Bob, I was just thinking about your top manager again. Somehow or other he has got to understand that if his job is going to grow, there is no way he can continue to do it all himself, and the time and effort in teaching his people the skills he's got is really a long-term investment. In terms of specific action, we're building a team called a "planning council" at the moment, but beyond that we haven't gone into work teams in specific areas. Also I've got a lot of learning yet to do on that subject.

Covington: You have to make them think it is their idea, subtly giving it to them so they can get some self-satisfaction from coming to the realization.

Farrell: I'm a little uncomfortable with that. If it really is their idea, O.K., but I don't want to be manipulative.

Covington: I agree with you that you don't want to be unreal in this, but unfortunately—maybe manipulative is not the right word—you certainly have to do some shaping. Maybe it's facilitating—you are planting a seed.

Kruel: I have a question regarding manipulation. Time and time again you hear a negative connotation, and I often wonder about this because quite often skilled managers do manipulate, by my definition, but they manipulate for "good". I guess it can have some pretty severely negative aspects—nobody likes to be manipulated.

Covington: Right. It's the kind of connotation we get traditionally that gives the uncomfortable feeling. Use another word: assisting, coaching, or facilitating.

Page: Facilitation, or the facilitator, is involved in a "win-win" situation with the other person. The manipulator, keeping the negative connotation, is involved in a "win-lose" situation with another person. In other words, he's going to win, the other person is going to lose. I guess I'll say that when we manipulate people, that's exactly what we have in mind—our own advantage. If we were facilitating we might be doing some of the same kinds of actions the manipulator would do, but it's a win-win situation—we're both going to win.

Kruel: Thanks for clarifying.

Farrell: I think Walt has identified one of the key questions; that is, you try to facilitate and the result you get isn't the result that you want. The question is: To what extent do you become directive in achieving the results that you want?

Kruel: I've got an interesting example. This one dealt with organization change. I think how you change or how you establish the original organization can be very, very critical. This one is more in the line of coaching or facilitating. I had to make an organization change and there were four men working for me at the time, each a department manager, each expecting to be moved up. I found that I had done a good job of having them look at their future potential. I tried to understand how each of them would react, and I knew I had a pretty significant problem, so the method I used to work the problem was critical. First of all, I wanted to hold onto everybody because I felt that this one step was only one step and there would be other opportunities which some of these men would fill. So I had an organization chart prepared, and one of the chaps came into my office and I struggled to hide what I had without being too obvious. But then I knew the individual, and knew that whatever he sees he's going to talk about. So I decided then and there that I would let him see the chart, indicating how I wanted to restructure. He went out and promptly told everybody, and the first man came in —a very proud individual, very capable—and said, "I hear you're going to reorganize and I'm not getting the job, and I want to tell you right now I'm quitting." So I said, "Okay, we've worked together for a long time. I thought we were friends. If you're going to make any move of that type without realizing that whatever the move is it's a very difficult one to make, and one that requires different skills and different guys that are all qualified, go ahead." He said he'd go home and talk to his wife about it.

The second man came about five o'clock and he was soused and promptly told me the same thing. "I quit. I thought I'd been loyal . . . ," and so on. I said, "Why, if you feel that way, fine, go ahead and quit." He said, "I might not be in tomorrow." I said, "Well, if you feel that way . . . but first, just go home and think about it." I finally got him out of there.

The next morning the third guy came up to me and said, "Boy, I suppose you've heard how I've been smarting off and being a damn fool about this. Forget it, whatever I said, I've been a damn fool about all of this." I had not heard anything. The one who was smashed came in and said, "Boy! I bet I made a fool of myself again." And I said, "No, I can understand the pressures." The last one, who was the toughest one, came in and said, "You know, my wife told me just what you told me." What happened, when I thought about it, was that it gave everyone an opportunity to come and quit and make whatever rash statements they wanted to make, but they also had an opportunity to retract and when they did that then they had committed themselves. From that point on the acceptance was developed. That worked very well.

I had another move, a very similar scenario, except it involved having to change the organization because we had problems not getting the work done—certain guys were skilled in some areas but critical of others, that type of situation. In this case we had regular sessions where we exchanged our progress and activities and such, and I thought it might not be a bad idea to talk about this reorganization with this group. Somewhere during the meeting I told them the subject matter and mentioned that it might be smart to look at this from the standpoint of reorganization. I went up to the board and started in drawing large blocks and said, "Let's just forget the functions we have, let's talk about how this thing can operate." I'd start with a function and somebody else would come up with something else, and it got to be very receptive of the political needs of the individuals, but at the same time I had to understand what the organization needed. We went through that process for several hours and we eventually ended up with an organization that pleased me very much, and it also moved individuals into appropriate areas. For instance, one man was in planning. He was not trained in quality control, and we had a very strong quality control organization. But the planning organization was very weak primarily because he did not have interest in planning. He had leveled off and didn't care for that as much as he used to. He didn't find it an exciting thing and he was very critical of quality control. He found many things needed to be improved in quality control. So, guess what happened? He talked himself into the quality control job, not only personally, but the other group members accepted it as well because they felt he had good ideas about how to improve. That was a relatively classic situation. I did reflect on a couple of things that came out. One, the idea of patience, and two, compassion and understanding of the drives of people that are involved. The one that is very significant that isn't discussed very much is controlling your own human reaction; patience. You tend to direct yourself into the channel that you have a feeling for, and concepts and theories and all those logical matters get discarded. Thus it is very important to keep the human emotions under control and go through a calculated thinking approach to the solution to the problem instead of an emotional one.

Chilton: I'm indebted to you, Walt, for what you've just been saying. While you were talking it reminded me about a situation in which I was assigned a task of building a team, which was extremely difficult because of the personalities involved. This was something brand new that had never been done before. I wrote down the things that I had to do in order to make it successful. The task was to create some data on all the New York Stock Exchange-listed stocks and to provide it for publication. The data were to provide technical information to evaluate selections for purchase and sales. The people who would be involved would basically be a computer expert, a fundamental investment analyst, a salesman, an administrator, a secretary, and myself. So there were six of us and none of the people had worked together—all very independent people who had been selected in order to get this job done in three months and determine what the market was, what should go in this publication, and what the price should be. I found out in order to get the job done these were the things I had to do: One was a considerable amount of training in imparting my experience. We talked about working together in outlining where responsibility would be placed. The task was transferring the experience that I had to an application of sales which might work in convincing the salesman that he should at least listen to them, not necessarily accept them, but maybe use some ideas. In doing that I had what I call "effective task assignment." I had to ask him to evaluate the different sales techniques. Someone had given me these ideas and maybe he could use some of them. In our progress meetings (which was also another technique) we tried to have effective questioning about where we were and where we were going.

Page: I've just noted that that was a "feedback loop."

Chilton: That's right. My next statement was going to be leading into the development of an open atmosphere for feedback. Then the delegation of the different things that had to be done and providing an innovative environment where everyone can interject all their thoughts—brainstorming sessions. We talked it out, trying to be perceptive about who could do what on the task, discussing problems that everyone had, and then we talked about my position, and dealing with the fact that I like to do things myself. That's how I relate to a group. I'm often guilty of dominance, "delicate management surveillance."

Covington: I think I better give you one illustration too. This has some of the negative connotations of being manipulative. In the process of forming agencies, we are involved in elective offices in some instances. We formed the easy agencies first, which basically involved appointed officers, because I have much better control there. The Law and Justice agency which is the most recent agency formed was made up of courts of three levels, the sheriff, the district attorney, the public defender, and the probation officer. All these have to do with crime and people problems relating to crime and the court process. Most of them are elective officers, all except two, and all of them negative towards the agency concept itself although there has been over two years of indoctrination as we've moved in this direction. In trying to reach the point where we could form this agency in the least objectionable way possible, we had to try and work it out from a timing standpoint. We have five members of the Board of Supervisors, all of whom supported the agency plan. But one member, a dominant member, is very sensitive to the elective process and to elective officers. So I waited until he took his vacation and then approached the Board again on forming the Law and Justice agency. We talked about this agency originally as being headed by a "coordinator" because the courts are arms of the state. They are somewhat separate from the rest of the County operations and they have a lot of independence. So the action that we had to take in order to get this agency formed was to act very precipitously. I did have the support of the Chairman of the Board to follow the process which we followed. The Board said, "Yes, we're going to do this, and we're going to do it now. We're not going to call the person a 'coordinator', we're going to call him an 'administrator' because all the other agency heads are administrators." Monday morning we called in all the department heads involved and the presiding judge. We brought them into the Board Chairman's office (no other Board members were present), and just laid out the fact that we were doing this and that we were going to take that action that morning. Well, the reaction was negative naturally—they had been negative right along—and they asked that it not be taken. But we went into the Board session at ten o'clock and the Board took the action and adopted the ordinance as an emergency ordinance and it went into effect. Probably if we had not used this technique we would not have the agency today. Now there has been a lot of resistance that has gone along with this, and we still do not have real acceptance, but this occurred nine months ago and the agency has been operating. Gradually we're going to get the acceptance and support.

This is just one illustration of a technique that had to be used in order to accomplish the goal and it doesn't necessarily follow the team concept that you have expressed. But in order to accomplish the ultimate organizational process that we're after we have found it effective.

Farrell: I don't necessarily offer this as the ideal model and I don't know if it would work in every case, but it worked superbly in this case. Shortly after I joined the company, a senior executive died and we had the task of replacing him.

We had three senior department heads eligible for that position, all three equally competent, and we went about it in a rather different way. We shared that problem with all three of them and we went through a number of meetings with them. We had that team of three people trying to define exactly what the requirements of such a position were as objectively as they could, and evaluating the various skills that each one could bring to that position. Slowly but surely after a period of about five meetings it got to a point where they arrived at a consensus of which of the three of them ought to do it. It was a good decision but, more importantly, after the decision had been made, the cohesiveness of those three working as a unit was superb, with the other two having made a personal commitment of support. I'm sure it would not always work that way. But that really gets back to the question of how you go about getting people to put their own personal desires and needs into some sort of perspective when participating in a group and making group decisions.

Page: This subject is so much greater than we're going to be able to handle in this text, perhaps when we make it a graduate text we could put in greater detail. You've all given illustrations and, as you talk, I think of any number. For instance, one that I as manager had in the last year was when we changed the structure of Pepperdine School of Business and Management from having an undergraduate and graduate program director to having three area chairmen and a program director who in turn headed up all the program managers of each program. But it was the three area chairmen who especially needed to function as a team. All had doctorates, all were professors, one of whom was the graduate director of programs and the other two men had been selected to fill the other two positions. Essentially the decision for the structure was mine, although there was consensus on the model as well as on the timing. I indicated that their task was to become a team. They spent hours together pounding out their differences and they've become an effective functioning team. I usually did not meet with them, but would go in for a half-hour session with them after they had met for three hours or so together. I made a point of not spending a whole lot of time with them. I spent limited periods of time with them, and they formed their own team.

Chilton: That's "delicate management surveillance"—knowing when to pull out, not spending all of your time with them because if you can get them to get the hard part out of the way first, then you're in a place to evaluate it.

Kruel: Another technique I found that is very valuable in team building is when quite often you do have people with dissimilar attitudes and opinions and the technique is to have them work on a problem or program where they must be involved in a very close relationship with each other to provide a common answer for something. There is always some trading off to find where the compatibility is. They can have dissimilar attitudes even about each other if that is in no way related to some common objective or goal.

Page: Dr. Ends and I wish to thank all of you. You have contributed immensely to our effort.